黄花梨文玩收藏集

黄继荣 编著

同济大学出版社·上海
TONGJI UNIVERSITY PRESS·SHANGHAI

序言一

应黄兄之邀,为其《黄花梨文玩收藏集》作序。

初识黄兄于甲午年(2014年)春,那时我亦玩亦商,经营"而立文玩"[1]已近三年,主打黄花梨雕刻,珠串和文房器物相对较少。黄兄喜欢收藏海南黄花梨民俗老物件,尤其木工手刨这一品类,他的一些藏品让我一饱眼福。为友数年,黄兄对黄花梨的珍爱一直未变,我们聊材质,聊工艺,聊收藏,互相交流、印证、学习。

黄兄曾游学欧洲及中美洲,但是,其最爱的始终是中国传统文化。两年前,黄兄便有将其藏品拍照成册、付梓成书的想法,与我谈及时,我认为这是一件非常好的事情。能将多年的珍藏拍照并整理成册,出版成书,既是总结、提升自我的一次机会,也是对黄花梨文玩很好的一次传播。

《黄花梨文玩收藏集》中收录了黄兄近年所藏的黄花梨物件,总计60件。种类涉及雕刻、文房、民俗老物件、摆件等,其中不乏精品佳作,材质、工艺堪称一流。令我印象最深的是《金玉满堂》。此摆件料质上乘,纹理迷人,降香浓郁,堪称越南黄花梨北方料的极品。无奈早期工艺水平受限,不免有浪费材料之嫌。黄兄同匠人几经构思讨论,在尽量减少材料损耗的前提下,将此件改制为"金玉满堂"这一传统题材。完工之际,我与黄兄感叹,真乃化腐朽为神奇的一件作品!

文玩无贵贱,品行有高低。马未都先生谈及黄花梨时曾经有这样一段论述:"我想黄花梨永远不会是大众使用的东西,它永远都是高端的,在历史上永远是中国的富裕阶层,而且是非常富裕的阶层才使得起。"我与黄兄当属平民百姓,并非中国的富裕阶层,但我们依旧喜爱黄花梨多年,在财力允许的前提下完成我们的收藏。古人云"君子如玉",而黄花梨相比其他木材最优质的特点也是温润如玉,所以黄花梨一直是君子之品。我想这也是我辈如黄兄喜欢黄花梨的真正原因吧。

黄兄于我亦师亦友,为其《黄花梨文玩收藏集》写序,实在不敢妄言,寥寥数百字,以表寸心。祝黄兄开心康健,吉祥如意。

琢物文玩 任博
己亥年 冬

---

[1] 作者注:而立文玩,又名"而立汇",由任博先生在其三十岁时创办于北京,专为紫黄木收藏爱好者提供专业服务,在国内圈内有口皆碑。2019年6月,"而立"正式更名为"琢物"。

序言二

理工科毕业的我原本与摄影并无太多交集。因为之前从事市场工作，经常涉及各类市场活动和宣传推广工作，不可避免地与广告公司和影视制作公司进行项目合作。在合作过程中，我发现视觉形象设计技能对于综合型的市场人员相当重要，因此在工作之余，开始学习平面设计和视频制作，在偶然的机会下又开始系统地学习摄影，并获得了国家摄影师二级技师资格证书。

同为复旦大学 MBA 专业的校友，数年前我与黄继荣先生在复旦大学的课堂相识。在分享本人摄影作品时，黄继荣先生提出了希望给自己多年珍藏的黄花梨藏品出版图册的想法。我俩一拍即合！

尽管之前拍过一些商业静物作品，但我对于文玩题材还是首次接触。这无疑是一次充满挑战的尝试。我对于商业静物拍摄的基本方法和拍摄流程有一定的把握，而黄继荣先生则对于黄花梨的鉴赏、收藏及其文化内涵有着自己独到的见解。就这样，我俩取长补短，通力合作，才有了今天呈现的效果。

任何一幅好的商业摄影作品都不太可能一蹴而就，除了需要对构图、布光、搭配等摄影基本要素准确把握和摄影基本技能的灵活运用外，更需要对被摄对象的特质、内涵甚至是文化有所理解。文玩题材更是如此！

此次有幸得到黄继荣先生的大力支持和帮助，使本人对于黄花梨收藏的基本知识、鉴赏等有了全新的认知。非常欣慰能为黄继荣先生的收藏集略尽绵薄之力，也衷心希望此次的摄影作品能给大家带来视觉上的享受。

对摄影感兴趣的朋友，也欢迎登录网站（http://www.jasonliangphotography.com）共同交流。

梁杰文
2019 年 12 月

目录

3	序言一	60	苦尽甘来
4	序言二	64	莲蛙
		68	灵猴捞月

上篇 雕件

		72	荷叶金蟾
		76	天子之玺
8	玉兰貔貅	80	金玉满堂
12	灵猴献瑞	84	如意灵芝
16	达摩坐禅	88	瑞芝仙草
20	代代封侯	92	苍龙教子
24	独占解元	96	生财有道
28	福寿灵芝	100	松鼠佛手
32	枯荷金蟾	104	母子金蟾
36	富甲天下	108	湍濑玄芝
40	招财金蟾	112	闻香悟道
44	荷叶貔貅	116	吴牛喘月
48	金蟾白菜	120	仙芝瑶草
52	母子貔貅	124	竹节貔貅
56	福至灵芝	128	夜夜数钱

目录

132	一路连科	188	酒瓶
136	一鸣惊人	190	仿古花瓶
140	鱼龙戏珠	192	木枕
144	知足常乐	194	擀面杖
148	参禅入定	196	文盒
154	三多佛手	200	帽筒
158	鱼跃龙门	202	虎皮纹花瓶
162	竹节蝙蝠	204	山水随形
166	祥龙戏珠	206	水波纹盘
170	醉卧达摩	208	镇纸
		210	薄壁山水纹花筒
	下篇 素器	212	茶台
		214	山水纹盘
176	石瓢壶	216	蒜头瓶
178	素笔筒		
180	黄花梨茶刀	219	参考文献
184	棋罐	220	后记
186	立柱		

上篇

雕件

玉兰貔貅

玉兰貔貅

长：6.5厘米　宽：4厘米　高：6.5厘米　重：25.8克　款：九品

咏玉兰

明·文征明

绰约新妆玉有辉，素娥千队雪成围。
我知姑射真仙子，天遣霓裳试羽衣。
影落空阶初月冷，香生别院晚风微。
玉环飞燕元相敌，笑比江梅不恨肥。

这件九品款的《玉兰貔貅》是由一块油性非常出众的老料所雕，其颜色深厚，木质细腻，棕眼全无。整件作品虽然体积偏小，却完美刻画了一只貔貅立于一朵玉兰花上，其构思巧妙，细节充沛，可谓巧夺天工。

貔貅，又称"辟邪"，是我国古代传说中的一种通灵神兽。《小尔雅·广言》中说："辟，除也。"顾名思义，是人们希望借助它的法力，驱走邪秽，破除不祥。《急就篇》中载有："射魃辟邪除群凶。"唐颜师古注曰："射魃、辟邪，皆神兽名……辟邪，言能辟御妖邪也。"

玉兰，别名"辛夷""木笔""玉堂春"，其素净怡人，芳香淡雅，在中国有着悠久的历史。《楚辞》中就有"朝饮木兰之坠露兮""辛夷车兮结桂旗""结桂树之旖旎兮，纫荃蕙与辛夷"等描绘玉兰的名句。在过去的江南宫廷庭院中，玉兰是一种名贵的观赏花卉，其花朵艳丽怡人，树形婀娜，枝繁花茂，无论孤植或丛植都很美观。

玉兰在现代一般有三种寓意。寓意之一是坚贞守护，"金兰之交"就是友情的最高层次，结拜之时也称"义结金兰"。寓意之二是感恩之心，玉兰花开放在碧绿的枝叶当中，花朵呈现无瑕的白玉之色，且一旦开放，就会散发出阵阵沁人心脾的香味，很多人认为玉兰花的美丽外表与香味，是为了感谢人们的细心栽培而奉献出来的，所以玉兰花代表一颗真挚的感恩之心。寓意之三是代表忠贞爱情，人们喜欢将它作为礼物送给自己所爱的人，而对方若是懂此寓意的话，就会瞬间明白其心意。

玉兰貔貅（局部）

Magnolia Pi Xiu

Length: 6.5 cm   Width: 4 cm   Height: 6.5 cm   Weight: 25.8 g   Sculptor: Jiu Pin

Singing Magnolia
By Wen Zhengming of the Ming Dynasty

Elegant and white, the magnolia is in full of bloom.
Seen from a distance, the flowers are like graceful beauties, dancing in snow-white dresses.
I think the magnolia must be from Gushe Mountain[1], from where they obtain such gorgeous dresses.
In the evening, the moonlight casts shadows of magnolia on the stone stairs,
And there is a pleasant aroma in the breeze.
Only two beauties, Yang Yuhuan and Zhao Feiyan, represent the magnolia's elegant temperament.
Even Jiang Caiping who had despised Yang cannot compare with the beauty of magnolia[2].

The oiliness of the aged material that was used to make the item, "Magnolia Pi Xiu", sculpted by Jiu Pin, is absolutely outstanding. It has a deep layer of color, and exquisite texture, with no flecks in the grain. Although the volume of the entire piece is small, it perfectly portrays a Pi Xiu standing on top of a magnolia flower. The design is delicate with abundant details, and the workmanship is superb.

The Pi Xiu, also called "Bi Xie" (meaning to ward off evil spirits), is a kind of mythological creature in ancient legends. *Guangyan of xiao Er ya* states, "It drives out and eliminates." As the name implies, it is the magical power which people hope to draw support from, to drive away demonic filth and eliminate inauspiciousness. *Jijiu Book* states, "The 'She Ji' wards off evil spirits and eliminates inauspiciousness." Notes by Yan Shigu says, "She Ji, Bi Xie, are all names of mythological creatures ... Bi Xie can repel evil spirits."

Magnolias, also called "Xin Yi", "Mu Bi", and "Yu Tang Chun", are simple, neat, and delightful. They are balmy and elegant, with a long history in China. The lines like "Drink the dew on magnolia in the morning", "Ride on the chariot made of magnolia trees with osmanthus branches as its flags", "I would love to wear perfumed bags made of osmanthus, as well as faber cymbidium and magnolia" are all famous sayings from *The Songs of Chu* that describe the magnolia. It was a kind of precious flower you could marvel at in the past Jiangnan courtyards. Whether a lone plant or a cluster, the trees are graceful with gorgeous and delightful flowers. They are all beautiful.

Modern magnolias normally have three kinds of meanings. The first is to protect, loyal to the end. "Intimate friendship" is the highest level of friendship. When you are sworn brothers, you can also be called close friends. The second is a graceful heart. Among the dark green leaves and branches of a blooming magnolia flower, the flower's white jade color appears flawless. Once it blooms, it sends out an aroma that refreshes the mind. Many people believe the beautiful appearance and aroma of the magnolia flower are to thank people for careful cultivation. As such, magnolia flowers represent a sincere and grateful heart. The third meaning is that it represents loyal and dependable love. People like to use magnolia flowers as a gift to the person they like. It expresses their strong love for that person. If understood, he or she will instantly be aware of their intentions.

---

[1] In many Chinese legends, Gushe Mountain is a place where beautiful female immortals live.

[2] Yang Yuhuan, Zhao Feiyan and Jiang Caiping who are famous for their beauty are all imperial consorts in Chinese history. However, Jiang despised Yang for her plumpness.

灵猴献瑞

灵猴献瑞

长：13厘米　宽：9厘米　高：8厘米　重：192.5克　款：三阳

感弄猴人赐朱绂
唐·罗隐

十二三年就试期，五湖烟月奈相违。
何如买取胡孙弄，一笑君王便著绯。

这件作品为三阳款《灵猴献瑞》，由一块油梨所雕，描绘的是一只灵猴背靠着三只仙桃，灵猴怡然自得，若有所思，仿佛在想如何品尝这些仙桃。

在中国传统文化中，猴子是常见的吉祥之物，为十二生肖中的一员，寄托着世人对自由和美好生活的向往。"猴"与"侯"同音，意味着升官封侯、飞黄腾达，而桃本身寓意长寿健康，二者互相配合，寓意吉祥，充满了世俗的谐趣美好之意。

石猴孙悟空在中国可谓是家喻户晓，其于人、仙、佛、妖四界周转，最后证道成佛的故事被世人一代一代传诵。其实猴子的佛缘原本就不浅，《师子月佛本生经》便生动记载了神猴被佛祖点化皈依的故事："如是我闻，一时佛住王舍城迦兰陀竹园，与千二百五十比丘、百菩萨俱。尔时众中有一菩萨比丘，名婆须蜜多，游竹园间，缘树上下，声如猿猴，或捉三铃作那罗戏。时诸长者及行路人竞集看之。众人集时，身到空中，跳上树端作猕猴声……八万四千金色猕猴集菩萨所，菩萨复作种种变现令其欢喜……时空泽中有一猕猴至罗汉所，见于罗汉坐禅入定。即取罗汉坐具披作袈裟，如沙门法偏袒右肩，手擎香炉绕比丘行。时彼比丘从禅定觉，见此猕猴有好善心，即为弹指告猕猴言：'法子，汝今应发无上道心。'猕猴闻说欢喜踊跃，五体投地，敬礼比丘。起复采花散比丘上，尔时比丘即为猕猴说三归依，告言：'法子，汝今随学三世佛法，应当求请受三归依及以五戒。'尔时猕猴即起合掌白言：'大德，忆念我今欲归依佛法僧。'"

佛经中多有与猴子有关的故事，且多认为猴子生性好动，象征心境不止，六根不净，而最终能将猴子收归佛门，也即显示佛门无槛，佛法无边。

灵猴献瑞
（局部）

A Monkey Offering Luck

Length: 13 cm   Width: 9 cm   Height: 8 cm   Weight: 192.5 g   Sculptor: San Yang

Thoughts About Buying a Monkey to Win an Official Post
By Luo Yin of the Tang Dynasty

For over a decade I have been taking the imperial exams for acquiring an official post but failed each time.
I left my hometown and was cut off from all the beautiful scenery.
I might as well buy a monkey to amuse the emperor,
Once the emperor felt pleased he may even bestow me a post.

This item is a San Yang sculpture of a "A Monkey Offering Luck". It was made from a piece of oily scented rosewood. It depicts a spirited monkey leaning against three peaches of immortality of Goddess Wangmu. The monkey has a strong and content manner. It looks pensive, seemingly thinking about tasting those peaches.

In Chinese traditional culture, the monkey is a commonly seen lucky animal. It is one of the twelve animals of the Chinese zodiac. It gives people hope for a free and beautiful life. "Monkey" (pronunciation is "hou" in Chinese) and "marquis" (also "hou") are homonyms. It signifies promotion, achieving meteoric success in one's career. The peaches signify longevity and health. Both fit each other, signifying luck and brimming with a secular meaning that is amusing and beautiful.

The Monkey King from *Journey to the West* is well-known in China. He rotates around four boundaries: man, immortal, Buddha, and creature. Ultimately, the story about of confirming Taoism and attaining enlightenment has been widely known from one generation to the next. In fact, the origin of monkeys in Buddhism is quite profound. *The Master Said About Jātaka* records the story of the monkey god being transformed by Buddha. "So I have heard, a Buddha once lived in Rajgir Kalandaka Venuvana with 1,250 Buddhist monks and 100 Bodhisattvas for a period of time. Once a Buddhist monk named Pasumi travelled to a bamboo garden. Suddenly there came voices from the trees which sounded like apes. The voices attracted the elders and those passing by to gather together and watch. He jumped on the tree and shouted just like the macaque ... Then 84,000 golden macaques gathered together and acted like bodhisattvas ... One of the macaques went to an arhat's residence and saw him. After he sat in meditation, it took the arhat's seat and wore kasaya. With its right shoulder bare, it held up an incense burner and walked around the Buddhist monk. Awaking from the meditation, the Buddhist monk thought it was kind-hearted, so he told the macaque at once that it should start the Buddhist path. The macaque heard this and became very excited. He kneeled down and bowed to the Buddhist monk. Then it sprinkled flowers to the Buddhist monk. The Buddhist monk said to the macaque that it should request to take refuge in the Buddha and observe five precepts. Then the macaque put his palms together devoutly and said, 'I will remember the rules and disciplines of Buddhism and hope to take refuge in the Buddha.'"

There are many stories about monkeys in the Buddhist scriptures, and most believe that monkeys are naturally active, which symbolizes that the mood is not stable, and the desire are not fully controlled. But the monkey can eventually be returned to the Buddhism, which means that the Buddhism has no threshold and the Dharma is boundless.

达摩坐禅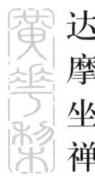

达摩坐禅

长：18厘米　宽：17厘米　高：16厘米　重：1034克　款：王集仪

达摩渡芦图（节选）

宋·刘克庄

长啸生风白浪起，高桅千尺如折箠。
佛狸百万不敢渡，师跣双髋踏一苇。
视鲁叟桴差简捷，比博望槎尤俶诡。
岂小儿女狡狯然，亦大神通游戏尔。
老胡西来纷文字，遍东西旦撒种子。
塔藏共礼熊耳骨，壁观谁得少林髓。

这件《达摩坐禅》取料于黄花梨糠梨树根料，由宁波工艺美术大师王集仪操刀而成。整件作品随形而制，周转圆润。达摩披巾而坐，炯目紧闭，面部纹理颇有风霜雕刻之感，左手边雕以一香炉，审美意义上契合整件作品的主题，又能实用做香插。而右边则刻有作者落款及创作年份，以及主题"悟"，颇见作者布局之精妙、手艺之神工。

通常雕刻取材海南黄花梨时，只伐取树干部分而把树根留在土壤里。其原因主要是：一来掘根颇耗费人力；二则动树根必会松动土层，破坏山体。因此海南的山中多埋有黄花梨树根。当后来黄花梨价格暴涨，成品的树木较为有限，世人便想到了开采以前弃之不用的树根，以资补市场。由于黄花梨油性饱满，埋在地里多年亦完好无损，且根本料质紧实，多是高密的紫油梨，实是创作海黄文玩的极品，由此曾经爆发过一场巡山挖掘海黄树根的运动。但毕竟资源有限，不出几年，整个海南山野间的海黄树根被挖掘一空，市场上能见到的海黄树根又日渐稀少起来。

达摩坐禅（局部）

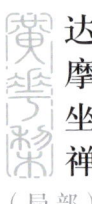

Meditating Dharma

Length: 18 cm   Width: 17 cm   Height: 16 cm   Weight: 1,034 g   Sculptor: Wang Ji Yi

A Picture of Bodhidharma Crossing with Reeds (Excerpts)
By Liu Kezhuang of the Song Dynasty

The whistling winds rolled up the layers of white waves,

The mast towered as if it were a cane.

Thousands of troops from the northern nomads were afraid to cross the river.

Yet Bodhidharma, with nothing but a pair of grass shoes, crossed on reeds.

The small bamboo and wood valve ridden by Confucius was not as convenient as those reeds,

The boat of Duke Bowang was not as unique as it was.

Common people saw it as a trick, indeed it is the great wisdom of sages.

He brought the Buddhist scriptures of South India,

Spread Buddhism seeds everywhere.

His body was shrined in a stupa.

However, who finally got the essence of his teaching in the Shaolin Temple?

The item, "Meditating Dharma", was made from dry scented rosewood, carved by the Wang Jiyi, a Ningbo (in Zhejiang Province) arts master. The entire piece was sculpted to fit its natural shape. It is mellow and full all around, with the Dharma wearing a shawl and sitting down. His bright eyes are closed tightly. The grain lines in his face are carved in such a way that gives him a very weather-beaten feeling. A censer is carved into the left-hand side. Its esthetic sense conforms exactly with the theme of this piece. It also serves a practical use for incense. The right side has the inscription of the sculptor's name and the year it was made, as well as the theme "epiphany". It is a very exquisite arrangement by the sculptor and the craftsmanship is amazing.

Normally when people collect Chinese scented rosewood for a sculpture, only part of the trunk is cut off, leaving the tree roots in the soil. The main reason is that: firstly, digging up roots is a waste of manpower; and secondly, moving tree roots can cause the loss of a layer of soil, destroying the form of the mountain. As such, there are many Chinese scented rosewood tree roots buried in the mountains of Hainan. Afterwards, the price of rosewood scented items increased sharply. Products made from the trees are fairly limited. People then thought of extracting the tree roots that were not needed and left previously. At the same time, due to the oiliness of scented rosewood being quite high, the roots buried for many years in the ground were still in good condition. Furthermore, purple oil scented rosewood tends to be quite dense. It is truely the best quality to create Chinese scented rosewood collector's items. There was once a big movement to patrol the mountains and dig up the Chinese scented rosewood tree roots. However, the resources were limited. Within a few years, entire mountains and fields of Chinese scented rosewood tree roots were excavated in Hainan Province leaving none left. The Chinese scented rosewood tree roots in the marketplace become fewer and fewer day by day.

代代封侯

代代封侯

长：9厘米　宽：6厘米　高：5.5厘米　重：73.3克

岭猿
唐·常建

杳杳袅袅清且切，鹧鸪飞处又斜阳。
相思岭上相思泪，不到三声合断肠。

猴，十二生肖之一，在《山海经》与《吕氏春秋》中被称为"猿"。《楚辞》尚有"猕猴"记载，四大名著之一的《西游记》中孙悟空就是一只石猴，而印度教亦有既是医神，又是勇士的神猴哈努曼。

这件作品整体塑型取之于"猴"的谐音"侯"和"袋"的谐音"代"，寓意着代代封侯。中国古代的官宦之家，倘若子孙后代不争气，再如何显赫亦难富贵过三代，要想破此局面，最好的方法便是求得一席爵位，封侯之后世袭，祖孙后代便能代代"吃皇粮"，所以封侯是古时士人的终极奋斗目标。

在这种文化背景下，古代的艺术文化造型出现了大量的寓意为封侯的作品，如画家常把猴子和马画在一起，取"马上封侯"之谐音与吉意。除此之外，"枫"也与"封"同音，也常与猴子画在一起表示"封侯"之意。猿猴同时还是长寿的象征，寓意延年益寿，因此也与青松、仙鹤常常同时出现在一幅画中。

代代封侯（局部）

Nobility Generation after Generation

Length: 9 cm   Width: 6 cm   Height: 5.5 cm   Weight: 73.3 g

Monkeys in the Mountain
By Chang Jian of the Tang Dynasty

From the distance, the voice of the monkeys is clear and sorrowful,
Partridges are flying under the sunset.
Weeping in the lovesick mountain with the tears falling down,
The lovesick heart has been broken with the crying of monkeys.

The monkey is one of the twelve animals of the Chinese zodiac. It was called an ape in *The Classic of Mountain and Sea* and *The Spring and Autumn of Lü Buwei*. Yet, it was recorded as a macaque in *Song of Chu*; Sun Wukong in *Journey to the West*, one of the four classic novels of Chinese literature, is a stone monkey. Hinduism, on the other hand, writes the sacred monkey, Hanuman, as both a warrior and a god of medicine.

This entire piece is modeled after a phrase wishing you good fortune "Dai Dai Feng Hou" means "nobility generation after generation". The word for monkey "hóu" and nobility in this phrase are homonyms. The word for bag, "dài" and "generation" are also homonyms. Therefore, the item implies the meaning of wishing you a good fortune. In ancient China, providing that the offspring's later generations were a disappointment, it was difficult for illustrious families to pass three generations with riches and honor. If you wanted to think about how to break this, the best method was to try to obtain nobility. After obtaining nobility, the title could be inherited. The generation following the grandchildren could then serve as government employees generation after generation. As such, nobility was the objective ancient scholars ultimately strived for.

Under this kind of cultural background, a large amount of ancient cultural pieces of art were designed to signify nobility. Such as artists often painting monkeys and horses together, using homonyms of the phrase "soon nobility" to wish one good fortune. In addition to this, maple tree (pronunciation is *fengshu*) and "feng" (the character in "fenghou" which means nobility) are homonyms. They are also often drawn together with monkeys to indicate the meaning of nobility. Apes and monkeys, at the same time, are a long lived symbol implying prolonged life. As such, they commonly appear together in paintings with pine trees and red-crowned cranes.

独占解元

独占解元

长：5.8厘米 宽：4.2厘米 高：2.5厘米 重：19.4克 款：立人

螃蟹咏
清·曹雪芹

桂霭桐阴坐举觞，长安涎口盼重阳。
眼前道路无经纬，皮里春秋空黑黄。
酒未敌腥还用菊，性防积冷定须姜。
于今落釜成何益，月浦空余禾黍香。

这件小品，是立人款的《独占解元》，描绘的是一只螃蟹趴于一只贝壳上。小螃蟹目炯筋健，神色矫然，行于方寸之间，气势不凡却又不失可爱。解元是明清两代时科举考试乡试的第一名，因为"解"与"蟹"谐声，此作寓意为乡试摘魁。

古人给蟹取"四名"："以其横行，则曰螃蟹；以其行声，则曰郭索；以其外骨，则曰介士；以其内空，则曰无肠。"由此蟹便有了"横行介士"和"无肠公子"的美称。

《夷坚志》记载："绍兴二年（1132），两浙进士类试于临安，湖州谈谊与乡友七人，谒上天竺观音祈梦，谊梦人以二楪贮六茄为馈，恶之。惟徐扬梦食巨蟹甚美，追旦，同舍聚坐，一客语及海物黄甲者，扬问其状，曰：'视蟳蜅差小，而比螃蟹为大。'扬窃喜，乃以梦告，人以为必中黄甲之兆。洎榜出，六人皆不利，扬独登科。"可见螃蟹自古便被寄托了万千士人于科举考试中夺魁的美好愿望。

独占解元（局部）

Alone at First-place

Length: 5.8 cm   Width: 4.2 cm   Height: 2.5 cm   Weight: 19.4 g   Sculptor: Li Ren

Crabs
By Cao Xueqin of the Qing Dynasty

We sit, cups raised, in the shade of osmanthus and Wu-tung;

Mouths watering, for the Double Ninth we pine

It crawls sidewise because the ways of the world are crooked,

And, white and yellow, harbors a dark design.

Wine won't purge the smell without chrysanthemums,

And ginger is needed dyspepsia to prevent;

What can it do now, fallen into the cauldron?

On the moonlit bank all that remains is the millet's scent.

This item is a Li Ren model of "Alone at First-place". It depicts a crab lying on top of a shell. The little crab is healthy. Its eyes are bright, and its expression is strong. It crawls in the small corner. Its grandeur is extraordinary, but it has not lost its cuteness.

"Jie Yuan" is the name for the top scorer in the imperial examinations during the Ming and Qing dynasties. Because "jie" sounds similar to "xie" (the Chinese word for crab), crabs signify that one will do outstanding on the examinations.

People of ancient times gave crabs "four names": "It is called crab after its side-ways walk; it is called 'guo suo' after the sound of its walk; it is called 'armored soldier' after its exoskeleton; it is called 'intestineless' after its empty interior." From this, the crab obtained the monikers: "side-ways walking armored soldier" and "intestineless son of nobility".

Record of the Listener records, "In the second year of the Shaoxing Period （1132）, two Chin-Shih scholars, Tan Yi and Xu Yang, from Zhejiang Province, were going to take an imperial civil-service exam in Lin'an, Huzhou. One day, they and other five friends prayed together to the Avalokitesvara, hoping to get good results in the exam. That night, they all had a dream. Tan Yi and five other friends dreamed of awful food while Xu Yang dreamed of eating delicious king crabs. The next morning when they chatted together, one mentioned a kind of yellow-shelled seafood. Out of curiosity, Xu asked for more details. The friend told him, 'Although it is smaller than Scylla serrata, it is bigger than normal crabs.' Then, in exaltation, Xu told them what he had dreamt. Everyone believed the yellow-shelled crab in Xu's dream would bring him good luck. Indeed, when the exam results came out, Xu found that he was the only one among them who ranked high." It can be seen that a myriad of scholars, since ancient times, have put their hope of placing first in the imperial examination in the crab.

福寿灵芝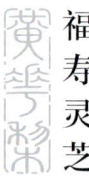

福寿灵芝

长：36厘米　宽：5厘米　高：9厘米　重：119.1克

步步娇·遍地有灵芝
宋·无名氏

遍地有灵芝。人人都不识。

作得业又大，难敌。

我今欲待说与你，只恐你不信，谈非。

这件《福寿灵芝》作品是海黄中性料所雕成，十朵灵芝并蒂开于一枝上，辅雕以一只蝙蝠，因此得名"福寿灵芝"。黄花梨中性料在文玩圈内并非上品，由于其成材年份不够，往往油性不足，但这件黄花梨中性料属个中罕见珍品，油性出彩，虎皮纹理，再加上精妙的雕工，寓意吉祥，不失为大方之作。

灵芝始载于《神农本草经》，称其"主耳聋，利关节，保神，益精气，坚筋骨，好颜色，久服轻身不老延年"。在中国古今的民间，灵芝始终颇受寻常人家的偏爱，以之能治"百病"，是神草仙药。同时在历代文人的笔下，灵芝也备受青睐，如我国历史上著名浪漫主义诗人屈原，其《九歌》中就提及"采三秀于山间"（"三秀"即灵芝），三国时曹植的《九咏》亦有"寻湘汉之长流，采芳岸之灵芝"的佳句。

古代传说中，"灵芝"被认为是瑶姬的化身。《山海经》中记载，炎帝的小女儿名叫瑶姬，刚到出嫁之年，就早夭离世，本是最美好的年纪，却只能"姑瑶之山，化为遥草"。之后世人借此传说，寄托以谁若是服下此"遥草"，便能与他（她）所思念的人在梦中相会的美好愿望。晋人习凿齿《襄阳耆旧传》和唐人余知古《渚宫旧事》亦均有记载，天帝哀怜瑶姬的早逝，封她为巫山云雨之神。这位美丽的女神，每天清晨化作一片朝云，自由清闲地徜徉在群峰之间；到了黄昏，又化作一阵阵暮雨，将她的一腔幽怨倾泻在千里长江之中。她的精魂散则为气，聚则为物。楚怀王有一次巡视云梦，住在高唐馆舍，这位女神来到寝宫，向正在酣睡的楚怀王倾诉爱情和哀怨。怀王从朦胧中醒来，无限怅惘，为纪念美梦，乃给瑶姬建立了一座庙宇，取名"朝云"。后来，楚襄王到此游览，也做了一个同样的梦，当时被传为佳话。楚国大文人宋玉乃根据这两个梦，写出了著名的《高唐赋》和《神女赋》。

灵芝形态别趣，曲线优美，自古以来除了作为世间万千画匠的绘画对象外，还常常被能工巧匠加工成艺术品，最常见的便是如意，其常被富贵之家当作华彩的装饰品，抑或作为官宦名门定亲之信物。

福寿灵芝（局部）

Lingzhi Mushrooms of Happiness and Longevity

Length: 36 cm   Width: 5 cm   Height: 9 cm   Weight: 119.1 g

Delicate Steps — Lingzhi Mushrooms Everywhere
By Anonymous of the Song Dynasty

Lingzhi mushroom sare everywhere but no one knows.
They're large and flat and hard to resist.
I wanted to tell you today, only I was afraid you would not believe, and say it is not so.

This piece, "Lingzhi Mushrooms of Happiness and Longevity", was carved from a neutral piece of Chinese scented rosewood. Ten lingzhi mushrooms sit atop the stem. In Chinese, the words "bat" and "happiness" have the same pronunciation. Therefore, a bat was added. Therefore, it is named "Lingzhi Mushrooms of Happiness and Longevity". Neutral scented rosewood isn't the top grade at the collector's items circle. Due to it not being aged, the oiliness often isn't sufficient. However, this neutral scented rosewood material is categorized as a rare valuable object. The oiliness is brilliant and it contains tiger fur-patterned veins. The workmanship is exquisite. The meaning behind it implies good fortune. It can be considered an expertly crafted piece.

Lingzhi mushrooms were recorded in The *Divine Farmer's classic of Materia Medica*. It states, "It helps to cure hearing impairment, maintain the joints, reserve the spirit, concentrate strength, and keep the face florid. It is also capable of promoting longevity if taken regularly in the long-term." People in ancient China and even today have been very partial towards lingzhi mushrooms, using it to rule over "every illness", as it is a magic medicinal herb. At the same time, the lingzhi mushrooms also received favor in the writings of scholars. China's famous romantic poet, Qu Yuan, in his poem *Nine Songs* mentioned lingzhi mushrooms: "Picking 'three blossoms' (lingzhi mushrooms — blossom three times yearly) in the mountains." During the Three Kingdoms Period (220–280), Cao Zhi in *Nine Chorales* also wrote the beautiful line, "Travelling along the Xiang River and the Han River while collecting lingzhi mushrooms grown on the bank."

In ancient legends, lingzhi mushrooms were believed to be the incarnation of Yao Ji (Chinese goddess). *The Classic of Mountains and Seas* states the Yan Emperor's (2000 B.C.) daughter was named Yao Ji. She passed away the same year she was able to be married. It was at the age when one was most beautiful. She was buried "in the Gu Yao Mountains, and turned into a medicinal herb". People of later generations pass down this legend which said that those who take the medicinal herb can meet together in a dream with the one he/she thinks of. Xi Zao Chi of the Jin Dynasty (265–420) in *Legends of Xiangyang* Shi and Yu Zhigu of the Tang Dynasty in *Affairs of the Zhu Gong* all wrote that a god had compassion for Yao Ji's early demise and offered her the deity of Mt. Wu's cloud and rain. This beautiful goddess turned into a morning cloud every morning, freely and idly wandering between the peaks of the mountains. At dusk, she turned into a burst of evening rain. She poured in torrents full of bitterness down thousands of miles long Yangtze River. Her spirit was scattered and evaporated, coming together to form an object. The King Huai of Chu (328 B.C.–299 B.C.) was once patrolling Yunmeng county in Xiaogan, Hubei Province. The goddess came down to his abode to the sleeping King Huai of Chu to tell him all of her romance and grief. King Huai awoke, hazy and in extremely low spirits. To commemorate his beautiful dream, he built a temple for Yao Ji called "morning cloud". Afterwards, the King Xiang of Chu (298 B.C.–263 B.C.) went sightseeing. He had the same dream again. At that time, this was a story that spread far and wide. The great scholar, Song Yu from the state of Chu, wrote the famous poems *Poems of Gaotang* and *Poems of the Goddess* based on these two dreams.

The shape of lingzhi mushrooms are particularly interesting, curving gracefully. Since ancient times, besides being used as the object for artists everywhere to paint, skilled craftsmen also frequently turn it into a work of art. The most commonly seen are quite satisfying. They are often turned into gorgeous ornaments in rich families or a keepsake for an official's marriage of a prestigious house.

枯荷金蟾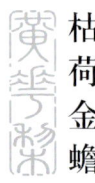

枯荷金蟾

长：14厘米　宽：7厘米　高：5厘米　重：46.2克　款：天工

棘隐壁（其二）
宋·白玉蟾

幽鸟噪岩谷，寒烟锁薜萝。
忽遇金蟾蜍，无人自呵呵。

这件《枯荷金蟾》材质为一块糠梨干料，原料中空，作者随物赋形雕作一朵枯荷，辅雕以两只小巧金蟾，相向而卧，细节巧妙，不失为一方精巧的案头小品。

金蟾亦称"三足金蟾"，是传统文化中典型的吉祥之物。三腿的蛤蟆方称"蟾"，世传其能吐钱，招财致富，源于"刘海戏金蟾"的传说，其有较多版本，此处仅举一例。

古时有位道士名刘海，拜吕洞宾和钟汉离为师，服侍两位神仙周游四海，降魔伏妖，布施造福人世。一日，他降伏了长年危害百姓的金蟾妖，彼时金蟾受伤断了一足，只余三足，自后金蟾拜服于刘海门下。为求将功赎罪，金蟾便使出绝活咬进金银财宝，助刘海造福世人，帮助穷人，发散钱财。世人念其功德，便逐渐将"刘海戏金蟾，步步钓金钱"的传说流传开来。

枯荷金蟾（局部）

Gold Frog on a Lotus Leaf

Length: 14 cm   Width: 7 cm   Height: 5 cm   Weight: 46.2 g   Sculptor: Tian Gong

Three Poems Written in the Mountains and Woods (2)
By Bai Yuchan of the Song Dynasty

The chirping of birds breaks the silent valley,

The chilly mist shrouds hermit's residence.

When I bump into a golden toad alone,

I burst into great laughter.

This "Gold Frog on a Lotus Leaf" is made from dry Chinese scented rosewood. The material is hollow. The sculptor carved a dry lotus leaf according to the object's natural shape. In addition, he added two delicate gold frogs lying down facing each other. The details are quite delicate. It is an elaborate piece to decorate one's desk with.

The gold toad is also called "the three-legged gold frog". In traditional culture, it is a typical creature of good luck. A three-legged frog is called "chan". Legend says it can spit up gold coins, inviting wealth. It originates from the story "Liu Hai and the Gold Frog". There are many versions to the story, one of which is given here as an example.

During ancient times, there was a Taoist priest named Liu Hai. He was paying respects to his masters Lyu Dongbin and Zhong Hanli. He was tending to the four seas travelling around the two immortals conquering demons and blessing the people. One day, he beat a gold frog spirit endangering the common people all year long. At that time the gold frog was hurt and one of its legs broke off. It was left with three legs. Afterwards, the gold frog yielded to Liu Hai and for atonement, the gold frog used a special power to spit out gold, helping Liu Hai bless the people, helping the poor, and dispersing the wealth. The people remembered his achievements and virtue. Gradually the legend of "Liu Hai playing with the gold frog and fishing money out step by step" was passed down.

富甲天下

富甲天下

长：13厘米，宽：11厘米，高：4厘米，重：124.8克，款：九品

螃蟹
宋·岳珂

无肠公子郭索君，横行湖海剑戟群。
紫髯绿壳琥珀髓，以不负腹夸将军。
酒船拍浮老子惯，咀嚼两螯仍把玩。
庐山对此眼倍青，原从公子醉复醒。

螃蟹是甲壳类，在科举时代象征科甲及第，解元是明清两代科考乡试的第一名，因为"解"与"蟹"谐声，寓意能够乡试摘魁。古代科举中有"一甲一名"之谓，暗喻及第登科，状元之才。当时科举有三甲之制，三甲之中以一甲最尊贵难得。蟹，有厚壳护身，犹如壮士披甲，故蟹被视为一甲的象征。其八只脚，能诸方攀涉，亦寓意八方来财、纵横天下、横财到手。《七修类稿》记载："阁老李西涯、学士程篁墩，成化间各以神童举于京。方朝见，适直隶贡蟹至焉，英宗即出一对试之，云：'螃蟹浑身甲胄'。程对曰：'凤凰遍体文章'。李对曰：'蜘蛛满腹经纶'。后西涯入相而经济天下，程则终于学士，以文章名世。"

在这种文化背景下，这件《富甲天下》出于传统却不囿于传统，独辟蹊径地以荷叶配以螃蟹，荷叶娉娉袅袅，螃蟹神采峻然，二者的结合互滋互补，取谐音寓意"和谐"，脱尘于世代传统，融入于时代面貌，可以说是传统文化和社会发展精妙的有机结合。

富甲天下（局部）

Abundance

Length: 13 cm   Width: 11 cm   Height: 4 cm   Weight: 124.8 g   Sculptor: Jiu Pin

Crabs
By Yue Ke of the Song Dynasty

Crab is a ducal son who makes a "guo suo" sound while crawling,
And runs amuck across the swords and spears in lakes and seas.
Purple whiskers, green shell, amber-colored bones,
And a belly like Zuo Zongtang.
Drinking and reveling on a boat,
Chewing and playing with the crab claws.
Even Mount Lu will turn green-eyed when seeing this.
Maybe it hopes to get drunk with me.

Crabs are crustaceans. During the period of imperial examinations, it symbolized passing the imperial examination. Jie Yuan was the first-place candidate in the preliminary round of triennial provincial imperial examinations during the Ming (1368–1644) and Qing (1644–1911) dynasties. Because "jie" sounds close to "xie (means 'crab')", it implies one is capable of doing outstanding on the imperial examinations. In the ancient imperial examiniations, they say "yi jia yi ming", a metaphor for the top scorer who passed the examination. At that time, the imperial examination had a three-rank system. Among the three ranks, the first rank (top three candidates) was the most respected and hardest to achieve. Crabs have a thick shell protecting the body, similar to a hero donning armor. Hence, crabs are regarded as a symbol of the top candidate. Its eight legs allow it to climb or wade in various directions. It also symbolizes fortune coming from all directions, being able to go at will and take possession of easy riches. *Qi Xiu Lei Gao* records, "Wen Yuan Ge Scholar Li Xiya and Han Lin Scholar Cheng Huangdun were both child prodigies famous across the capital in the Chenghua Period. When they went to meet the Emperor Yingzong, the crabs from Zhili Province were delivered to the palace. So the emperor made the first line of a couplet to test the two prodigies, 'crab, armed in heavy armor.' Cheng replied, 'phoenix, covered by beautiful patterns.' and Li replied, 'spider, full of silk threads.' Years passed, and Li Xiya became the prime minister to help govern the country, and Scholar Cheng came to be known for his excellent essays."

Under this kind of culture, this item stems from tradition, but is not limited to tradition. It displays originality by pairing a lotus leaf with a crab. A lotus leaf rises in spirals gracefully, and a crab is full of vigor and towering. The combination is nourishing and complimentary to each other. It dusts off generations of tradition by integrating with temporal appearances. Lotus leaf ("he ye") and crab ("pang xie") and harmony ("he xie") are homonyms. It can be seen as an exquisite, organic combination of traditional culture and the development of society.

招财金蟾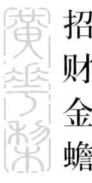

招财金蟾

长：20厘米　宽：8.5厘米　高：6.8厘米　重：80.6克　款：九品

无题二首（其二）

唐·李商隐

飒飒东风细雨来，芙蓉塘外有轻雷。
金蟾啮锁烧香入，玉虎牵丝汲井回。
贾氏窥帘韩掾少，宓妃留枕魏王才。
春心莫共花争发，一寸相思一寸灰。

这件《招财金蟾》作品描绘的是三只金蟾卧于荷叶之上，其中两只口衔一串钱币，寓意着招财进宝、财源广进。

这里要讲另外一个"刘海戏金蟾"的版本。"刘海戏金蟾"，人物原型出自后梁燕山，其间有位姓刘名玄英的读书人，原名操，号海蟾，字宗成。此人好谈性命，崇拜黄老之学。传说刘海蟾两次遇到神仙，第一次遇到"正阳祖师"，第二次遇到"吕祖"，据《神仙通鉴》记载："初遇正阳祖师，授以金液还丹之旨，遂弃官学道，后遇吕祖，乃改名玄英号海蟾子，复授以金丹之要，遁迹终南，修真成道。"有人说他是道教北宋第四祖，元代至元年间被封为"明悟弘道真君"，武宗时加封为"纯佑帝君"。有古籍说他是后梁广陵（今河南息县）人，也有说他是后梁陕西人。据说，有一天一位自称"真阳子"的道人前来拜访，和他大谈"一生二，二生三，三生万物"的"道"，海蟾终于大彻大悟，弃官学道，遁迹终南山下，丹成后登入仙班，化鹤而去。道教南宗把他奉为祖师，正阳道人就是钟离祖师，吕祖指的是吕洞宾。吕洞宾是传说中的八仙之一，号"纯阳子"，他因科举不第而浪迹江湖，遇到了"正阳子"钟离权，钟离权赠与他丹诀，并把他带到终南山修道，吕洞宾和刘海蟾应该算是师兄弟的关系。后人把刘海蟾这个名字一分为二：刘海、金蟾，又把这两个名字敷演为"刘海戏金蟾"。

这个故事跟刘海降伏金蟾的故事大相径庭。首先是刘海和吕洞宾的关系不同，一个是师父和徒弟，一个是师兄和师弟；其次是金蟾的寓意不同，一个金蟾是妖，被刘海降伏，另一个是根本没有金蟾，金蟾的"蟾"本身就是刘海自己。而哪个版本更真实，就是见仁见智的事了。

招财金蟾（局部）

Gold Frogs Iniviting Wealth

Length: 20 cm   Width: 8.5 cm   Height: 6.8 cm   Weight: 80.6 g   Sculptor: Jiu Pin

Two Poems Without Title（2）
By Li Shangyin of the Tang Dynasty

The east wind blows and the rain drifts. Above the beautiful lotus pond come bursts of gentle thunder.
The golden toad bites the lock-shaped incense burner with refreshing fragrance,
And the jade-tiger-shaped pulley draws the rope to get the well water.
Jia peeked through the curtains at handsome young Han Shou with her heart beating.
Imperial Concubine Mi presented Cao Zhi with a jade pillow to express her admiration for his literary style.
I yearn for a good love that does not fight with the blooming spring flowers,
Lest my lovesickness turn to ashes.

This work, "Gold Frogs Inviting Wealth", depicts three gold frogs lying on a lotus leaf. Two of the frogs have a string of coins in their mouths. It means that they are ushering in wealth and prosperity and numerous resources.

Here we will discuss an additional version of the story of "Liu Hai and the Gold Frog". The character in "Liu Hai and the Gold Frog" is from Yan Mountains of Later Liang (907–923). In the story there is a scholar named Liu Xuanying. His original given name was Cao and he styled himself as Haichan. He understood life and the Yellow Emperor school of thought. Legend says Liu Haichan had met an immortal twice. The first time, he met "Founder Zhengyang" (also known as "Zhongli Quan"; one of the Eight Immortals). The second time, he met "Founder Lyu" *Common Evaluation of Immortals* recorded, "The first time meeting Founder Zhengyang, he was taught about making pills of immortality and abandoning academic intuition. Afterwards, he met founder Lyu. He changed his name from Xuanying to Haichan and again taught about pills of immortality, leading a hermit's life in Zhongnan Mountains, and training to attain illumination." Someone said he was the fourth forefather of Taoism in the Northern Song Dynasty. In Zhiyuan Period of the Yuan Dynasty, he was given the title by the emperor as Mingwuhongdao Emperor. During the Wuzong Period, he was given the title of "Pure Emperor". Some ancient texts said that he is from Houliang Guangling (Xi County in Xinyang, Henan). Others said he is from Houliang Shaanxi Province. It is said that one day someone calling himself "Zhen Yangzi" came to pay a visit and harangued him with the teachings of "Of one are born two, of two are born three, of three are born all living things." At last Haichan achieved epiphany. He abandoned academic institution. He went to live as a hermit beneath Zhongnan Mountains; and after making the pills, he became immortal, turned into a crane and left. The Taoists southern Sect gave him the title of forefather. The Taoist, Zhengyang, is the forefather, Zhongli. Founder Lyu refers to Lyu Dongbin. Lyu Dongbin is one of the Eight Immortals from legends. He is called "Chun Yang Zi". Because he failed the imperial examinations, he roamed far and wide and met "Zheng Yang Zi" Zhongli Quan. Zhongli Quan gave him the secrets of making pills of immortality and took him to Zhongnan Mountains to practice Taoism. Lyu Dongbin and Lin Haichan ought to be considered fellow apprentices. Later generations divided his name into two parts: Liu Hai and Jin Chan (the latter meaning gold frog). They then made these two parts into the story "Liu Hai and the Gold Frog".

This story is quite different from the story of "Liuhai subduing the gold frog". First, Liu Hai's relationship with Lyu Dongbin is different. In the latter story they're master and apprentice, while in the former one they're the senior and the junior apprentice. Moreover, the meaning of the gold frog is different. In the latter story the gold frog is a spirit subdued by Liu Hai, while in the former one there is no gold frog. The "frog", that is, "chan", is Liu Hai himself. No matter which version is true, everybody's opinion differs on the matter.

荷叶貔貅

荷叶貔貅

长：6.5厘米　宽：7.5厘米　高：4.2厘米　重：108.1克　款：九品

貔貅出世

三代神器夏商周，龙生九子名貔貅。

铜铁炉中翻火焰，几千寒暑几春秋？

这件作品名为《荷叶貔貅》，刻画的是瑞兽貔貅卧在荷叶之上，貔貅的雄峻搭配荷叶的娉婷，皎皎然有神美之姿。

"貔貅"为中国传统文化中有名的神兽，又名"辟邪""天禄"，寄托着招财进宝的美好愿望。其传统形象为口大无肛，神威浮于脸上，喜金银珠宝的味道，只进不出，忠心护主，在传统文化中它是与龙和麒麟并称的瑞兽，均非世间之物。据神话记载，貔貅为龙王所生九子中的第九子，曾助轩辕黄帝于涿鹿之战中大败大巫蚩尤。而在正史中，也出现过貔貅的身影。《汉书·西域传》记载："乌戈山离国有桃拔、狮子、犀牛。"孟康注曰："桃拔，一曰符拔，似鹿尾长，独角者称为天禄，两角者称为辟邪。"《逸周书·周祝》："山之深也，虎豹貔貅何为可服？"《史记·五帝本纪》："（轩辕）教熊罴貔貅䝙虎，以与炎帝战于阪泉之野。"

此外，古人也多用貔貅比喻勇猛的战士。唐朝张说的《王氏神道碑》载有："赳赳将军，貔貅绝群。"清时毕著《纪事》诗："乘贼不及防，夜进千貔貅。"同时近人柳亚子《读史》诗之七亦有句："绿林家世拥貔貅，乳臭儿郎据上流。"

荷叶貔貅
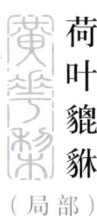
（局部）

Pi Xiu on a Lotus Leaf

Length: 6.5 cm   Width: 7.5 cm   Height: 4.2 cm   Weight: 108.1 g   Sculptor: Jiu Pin

The Birth of Pi Xiu

A treasured sword was passed through Xia, Shang, and Zhou Dynasties,

And Dragon King's ninth son is called Pi Xiu—the beast of fortune and wealth.

The sword is cast in the bronze and iron furnace,

Through thousands of years it is finally built.

This item is called "Pi Xiu on a Lotus Leaf". It portrays a Pi Xiu (a mythical animal that brings luck and wards off evil) lying on a lotus leaf. The Pi Xiu's imposing manner pairs nicely with the lotus leaf's grace. Their clear and bright disposition is both beautiful and mysterious.

The Pi Xiu is a mythological creature in Chinese traditional culture. It is also known as Bi Xie (mythical lion-like animal that wards off evil) and Tian Lu (like Bi Xie, but resembles a deer with two horns and a long tail). People hope that they could usher in wealth and prosperity. Traditionally, its image is portrayed with a large mouth and no anus. The deity's power is in its face, with a hint of a fondness for treasure. It doesn't let go of the treasure and faithfully protects the owner. In Chinese culture, it is a combination of the "long" (dragon) and "kylin" (Chinese unicorn), none of which is of this world. According to the legend, Pi Xiu is the ninth offspring of Dragon King. It helped Yellow Emperor, Yuan Xuan, defeat the great shaman, Chi You, in the battle of Zhuolu. However, Pi Xiu's figure has appeared in history. *Annals of the Western Region* in *Chronicles of the Han Dynasty* writes, "In Wuge Mountain in the Shu Kingdom, there are Taoba, lions, and rhinoceros." Meng Kang stated, "Taoba, called Fu Ba, resembles a deer with a long tail. The single horned one is called 'Tian Lu'; the two-horned one is called 'Bi Xie'". *Yizhou Shu - The Teachings of People* writes, "The mountains are so deep and remote, how can tigers, leopards, and other ... get accustomed to this." *Records of the Historian - Biographic Sketch of Five Emperors* also describes Pi Xiu wonderfully, "(Yuan Xuan) Teaching bears, Pi Xiu and other beasts about tactics so that they can fight Yan Emperor in the battle of Banquan."

In addition, people of ancient times more often used Pi Xiu figuratively to mean a brave and fierce warrior. Zhang Shuo of the Tang Dynasty in *Wang's Tombstone* writes, "As a majestic general he stands out and goes beyond his peers." Bi Zhu of the Qing Dynasty wrote in his poem *Chronicles*, "Thousands of brave troops attacked the enemies at night when they have not been prepared for guarding against such attack." At the same time, Liu Yazi's seventh poem in *Reading History* also has a line that writes, "The warrior has a group of brave young Pi Xiu (soldiers), who occupy the upper society."

金蟾白菜

金蟾白菜

长：22.5厘米　宽：16厘米　高：7.5厘米　重：462克

种菘
宋·方岳

老圃相传秋后菘，砖炉石铫一年冬。
宁知迟种迟於我，又见南薰上番风。

　　这件《金蟾白菜》海黄雕，雕工精美，寓意祥瑞，是我最钟爱的几件作品之一。

　　黄花梨的生长极缓慢，十年温养，甲子树型，百年方能成材。黄花梨的心材称为"格"，只有"格"在雕刻时方能为我所用。成熟的黄花梨根据心材颜色和质地，主要分为糠格和油格，油格颜色深、密度大，糠格颜色浅、密度小。这件《金蟾白菜》的料质并不十分特殊，只是糠格、油格相间的地方，看上去深浅交互，是为糠格和油格相互转换之处，实为点睛之笔，如道家的阴阳太极相生图，浑然天成，尽显风采。其上辅雕有两只三足金蟾，口衔一串钱币，炯然标致，寓意招财进宝。

　　白菜最早称为"葑"，后来经选育，千古演变，方成为如今品相，称为"菘"。《诗经·谷风》中有"采葑采菲，无以下体"的记载，意味着距今三千多年前的中原地带，其已相当普遍。而到了秦汉时期，吃起来细腻而富有甜味的菘菜从"葑"中分化出来，彼时之人陶弘景说，菜中有菘，最为常食。等到唐朝，已选育出白菘，之后的宋朝正式称为白菜。北宋著名词人苏轼有诗曰："白菘类羔豚，冒土出蹯掌。"认为白菜的美味可以和熊掌、羊羔相媲美。范成大也曾作诗夸赞白菜说："拔雪挑来塌地菘，味似蜜藕更肥浓。"明代李时珍在《本草纲目》中引陆佃《埤雅》说："菘，凌冬晚凋，四时常见，有松之操，故曰菘。今俗谓之白菜，其色青白也。"可见古之文人对它的推崇。

　　白菜虽为一种古今常见的普通菜蔬，却屡屡出现在文学作品中，至于近代，更是以国画、玉雕等艺术形式广为流传，甚至有相当一部分艺术家对"白菜"热衷近乎痴迷。齐白石靠着非凡的画艺更是把白菜提升到百菜之王的地位，他有一幅写意的白菜图，其上题句曰："牡丹为花之王，荔枝为果之先，独不论白菜为菜之王，何也？"

　　白菜多为中国传统文人所重视的原因，主要是其与"百财"谐音，有聚财、招财、发财的含义。现存最著名的白菜艺术品当属中国台北故宫博物院的镇馆之宝《翠玉白菜》，其由翠玉雕琢而成，后人普遍认为是光绪皇帝妃子瑾妃当年入皇室时的嫁妆，价值连城，是为如今中国台北故宫博物院的镇馆之宝，极其珍贵。

金蟾白菜
(局部)

Gold Frog on Cabbage

Length: 22.5 cm   Width: 16 cm   Height: 7.5 cm   Height: 462 g

Growing Cabbage

By Fang Yue of the Song Dynasty

The old gardener knows that the post-autumn Chinese cabbage needs to be carefully cared for in the winter.
I know it grows so long before the spring wind blows again.

This Chinese scented rosewood carving "Gold Frog on Cabbage" is refined. It symbolizes luck and is one of the pieces I treasure the most.

Scented rosewood grows extremely slowly — ten years to cultivate and a cycle of sixty years to form a tree. You can use it after a hundred years. Scented rosewood pith is called "ge". I can only use "ge" for a carving based on the matured color and texture of the scented rosewood pith, mainly dividing into the oily pith and the dry pith. The quality of its material is not very special, but it displays the region where the oily pith and the dry pith alternate, appearing deep and shallow in turn. Where the dry pith and oily pith change is truly the brush stroke that dots in the eyes. Like the image of the Taoist "Yin" and "Yang", it resembles nature itself in the most conspicuous and elegant manner. The carving features two bright and pretty three-legged gold frogs, their mouths holding a string of coins. It symbolizes wealth and prosperity being ushered in.

Cabbage, at the earliest, was called "turnip" ("feng"). After developing over the ages, it became what it is now and is called "song". *The Book of Songs - Valley Wind* writes, "The entirety of song and fei turnips can be used." It implies it was already widespread three thousand years ago in the Central Plain region. During the Qin and han dynasties (221 B.C.–206 B.C. and 206 B.C.–220 A.D. respectively), however, the turnip dish that was exquisite and richly sweet came from the above mentioned "feng" (turnip). Tao Hongjing from that time period said, "The dish has song (cabbage). It is most commonly eaten." During the Tang Dynasty (618–907), seed selection brought out white "song". Afterwards, during the Song Dynasty (960–1279) it was formally called "bai cai" (cabbage: "bai" meaning "white", and "cai" meaning "dish" or "vegetable"). A poem of the famous poet, Su Shi from the Northern Song Dynasty, writes, "Snow-white cabbage is as tasty as lambs and pork, and comes out like bear paws." He believed cabbage's flavor matched well with bear paws and lamb. Fan Chengda also praised cabbage in his poem, "We removed the snow and selected the newly picked cabbage, which tastes as good as lotus root." Li Shizhen of the Ming Dynasty quoted Lu Dian in *Pi Ya* saying, "Cabbage withers in late winter. It is commonly seen in four seasons. It has characteristics of pine. It is called 'song'. Today, it is known as 'bai cai'." It can be seen that ancient scholars thought highly of the cabbage.

The cabbage, both then and now, is a commonly seen average vegetable. However, it appears over and over again in literature and, in modern times, more so in national paintings, jade carvings, and such widespread art. There is even a portion of artists who feel strongly about "bai cai". Qi Baishi used an unusual painting style, so much as to place the cabbage in a position as being the king of vegetables. He had one painting depicting the cabbage, and its inscription reads, "Peony is the king of flowers, litchi is the first of all fruits; regardless, cabbage is the king of vegetables."

The reason why many Chinese traditional scholars' value the cabbage is mainly because it has the similar homonyms with "numerous wealth" (also "bai cai"). It symbolizes an accumulation of wealth, an invitation of wealth, or to become wealthy. The most famous art pieces of the cabbage in existence belong to the Chinese Taipei Palace Museum's jade cabbage, sculpted from a bluish-green jade. Later generations commonly believed it was the dowry of Emperor Guangxu's concubine, Jin Fei, when she entered the royal family. It is invaluable, an extremely precious treasure guarded by Chinese Taipei's Palace Museum nowadays.

母子貔貅

母子貔貅

长：16厘米　宽：5厘米　高：4厘米　重：86克　款：百艺

满江红·万灶貔貅

宋·黄机

万灶貔貅，便直欲、扫清关洛。
长淮路、夜亭警燧，晓营吹角。
绿鬓将军思饮马，黄头奴子惊闻鹤。
想中原、父老已心知，今非昨。

狂鲵剪，於菟缚。
单于命，春冰薄。
政人人自勇，翘关还槊。
旗帜倚风飞电影，戈铤射月明霜锷。
且莫令、榆柳塞门秋，悲摇落。

　　这件百艺款紫油梨作品名为《母子貔貅》，由一块质地细腻的海黄紫油梨老料雕成，刻画的是大小两只貔貅，大貔貅回首凝望，神态逼真，小貔貅憨态可掬，楚楚动人，实为一件罕见的上乘之作。

　　相传貔貅是一种凶猛的瑞兽，雄性名为"貔"，雌性名为"貅"，分为一角和两角，一角称为"天禄"，两角称为"辟邪"。有一种说法认为，单、双角区别公（为貔）母（为貅），但总之貔貅单、双角都有，而今世人所见的多数都是单角貔貅，双角貔貅几乎绝迹。

　　古代人多喜用貔貅来指代勇猛的战士，京剧《失街亭·空城计·斩马谡》中诸葛亮曾有一句著名的唱词"各为其主统貔貅"，"貔貅"意指百万雄师。南宋词人黄机在《满江红·万灶貔貅》中亦用"貔貅"来比喻千军万马。

　　中国古代风水学者认为貔貅是转祸为祥的吉瑞之兽，从古至今，上自帝王、下至百姓都极度注重收藏和佩戴貔貅。传说中貔貅除了开运、辟邪的功效之外，还有镇宅、化太岁、促姻缘等作用，人们相信它能带来欢乐及好运。

母子貔貅（局部）

Mother and Child Pi Xiu

Length: 16 cm   Width: 5 cm   Height: 4 cm   Weight: 86 g   Sculptor: Bai Yi

Man Jiang Hong - Tens of Thousands of Pi Xiu
By Huang Ji of the Song Dynasty

Thousands of troops, in high morale, are determined to beat off the Jin people.

At night, the Song soldiers still keep careful lookout along the Huaihe River.

When the day dawns, horns will be blown.

The young Jin general is preparing to flee, and the yellow-headed Jin troops have lost their morale,

Frightened by the sound of the horn.

Our people who live on the central plain ensure the Jin's doom,

For our troops are much stronger than what they used to be.

The Jin will disappear from our land, as ice will melt when spring comes.

With bravery and courage, our Song troops are unstoppable.

The flag is fluttering and the blade is sharp.

The imperial court should recover the lost land so that the sight of willows growing

On the border will not arouse melancholy sentiments any longer.

This purple oil scented rosewood Bai Yi model is called "Mother and Child Pi Xiu". It was carved from a piece of aged purple oil Chinese scented rosewood with exquisite texture. It depicts two Pi Xiu (a mythical animal that brings luck and wards off evil, having a dragon's head and a lion's body). The adult Pi Xiu's head is turned and gazing behind. It has a lifelike appearance. The young Pi Xiu is charmingly naive, lovely and touching. It is truly a rare and first-class piece.

Pi Xiu has been passed on as a kind of fierce, auspicious animal. The male is called "Pi"; and the female is called "Xiu". They're divided into single-horned and two-horned ones. The single-horned one is called "Tian Lu", and the two-horned one is called "Bi Xie". There's a saying that the difference between the single-horned and two-horned ones is the male (Pi) and female (Xiu). However, in short, Pi Xiu includes both single-horned and two-horned ones. Now, the majority of people all see Pi Xiu as being single-horned. The two-horned Pi Xiu has almost vanished. Many people of the ancient times were fond of using Pi Xiu to mean brave and fierce warriors. In Beijing opera, *The Loss of Jieting - The Trick of Deserted City - The Death of Ma Su*, Zhuge Liang sings the famous line, "Each of Pi Xiu uniting for his master." The meaning of "Pi Xiu" implies millions of troops. The poet, Huang Ji of the Southern Song Dynasty, also used Pi Xiu to signify a magnificent army with thousands of troops in *Man Jiang Hong - Tens of Thousands of Pi Xiu*.

The ancient Chinese geomancy scholars believed that Pi Xiu was an animal that could turn calamity into luck. From ancient times until today, from the monarch to the common people, everyone likes to hoard and wear Pi Xiu objects. In legends, besides bringing luck and warding off evil spirits, Pi Xiu also guarded one's residence, promoting predestined marriage, etc. People believe it could bring gaiety and good luck.

福至灵芝

福至灵芝

长：7.8厘米　宽：5.5厘米　高：2.3厘米　重：17克　款：石争

腊月中游发生洞裴回之际见双白蝙蝠三飞洞门
唐·韦洪

欲验发生洞，先开冰雪行。
窥临见二翼，色素飞无声。
状类白蝙蝠，幽感腾化精。
应知五马来，启蛰迎春荣。
露冕闻之久，鸣驺还慰情。

这件作品主题为蝙蝠卧于一柄灵芝上，蝙蝠轻巧灵动，灵芝福瑞吉祥，因此得名《福至灵芝》。中国古代文化中，"蝙蝠"寓意着"遍福"，象征福祚绵延，庇佑世代。世人常说的"五福（蝠）临门"，其早期的表象图案就是由五只蝙蝠组成，最早载于《书经》和《洪范》。五福的第一福是"长寿"，第二福是"富贵"，第三福是"康宁"，第四福是"好德"，第五福是"善终"。中国古代的农耕社会，人的生存和六畜蓄息均依赖于天时，非人力之所能控，面向不可测的自然世界只有祈祷，并且试图托以吉祥的寓意庇佑现实生活和子孙世代，因此在传统文化中，蝙蝠绝对是"福"的象征，这在许多留存的古老建筑以及砖刻、石刻中几乎处处可以见到。

福至灵芝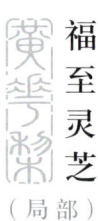（局部）

Good Fortune atop a Lingzhi Mushroom

Length: 7.8cm   Width: 5.5 cm   Height: 2.3 cm   Weight: 17 g   Sculptor: Shi Zheng

Seeing Two White Bats Flying When Traveling in the Fasheng Cave in the Middle of the Twelfth Month of the Lunar Year

By Wei Hong of the Tang Dynasty

I want to travel in the Fasheng cave,
So I managed to walk on icy and snowy roads.
When I observed the cave,
I found two white bats flying silently.
They looked like white bats, sensitive to the surroundings,
When they rose high into the air, they turned into spirits.
These insects know the prefecture chief is to visit here,
After a long hibernation they are awaken to greet the vivifying spring.
The competence of the prefecture chief has long been well-known.
He brings many entourages and gives comfort to civilians.

This item depicts a bat lying on a lingzhi mushroom. Bats are dexterous and quick-witted. Lingzhi mushrooms symbolize good fortune and luck. As such, it is named as "Good Fortune atop a Lingzhi Mushroom". In ancient Chinese culture, the Chinese word for bat "bian fu" implies "there is happiness everywhere" (also "bian fu"). It symbolizes continuous good fortune and blessings for many generations. People often say, "Five joys (bats) arrive home." (the word for joy/good fortune and bats are homonyms) The early representation was composed of five bats. The earliest recording was found in *Book of History* and *Grand Law* ("*Hong Fan*"). The first of five joys is "longevity", the second is "riches and honor", the third is "health and peace", the fourth is "goodness and virtue", and the fifth is "a good ending". In the ancient Chinese farming community, people's existence and the flourishing of the six domestic animals (pig, cow, sheep, horse, chicken, and dog) were equally dependent on the heaven's natural order, uncontrollable by human's strength. Faced with an unforeseeable nature, the world can only pray and attempt to commit lucky blessings to real life and offspring for many generations. Therefore, in traditional culture, bats are absolutely symbolic of "good fortune". This can be seen almost everywhere preserved in many ancient buildings, brick carvings, and stone inscriptions.

苦尽甘来

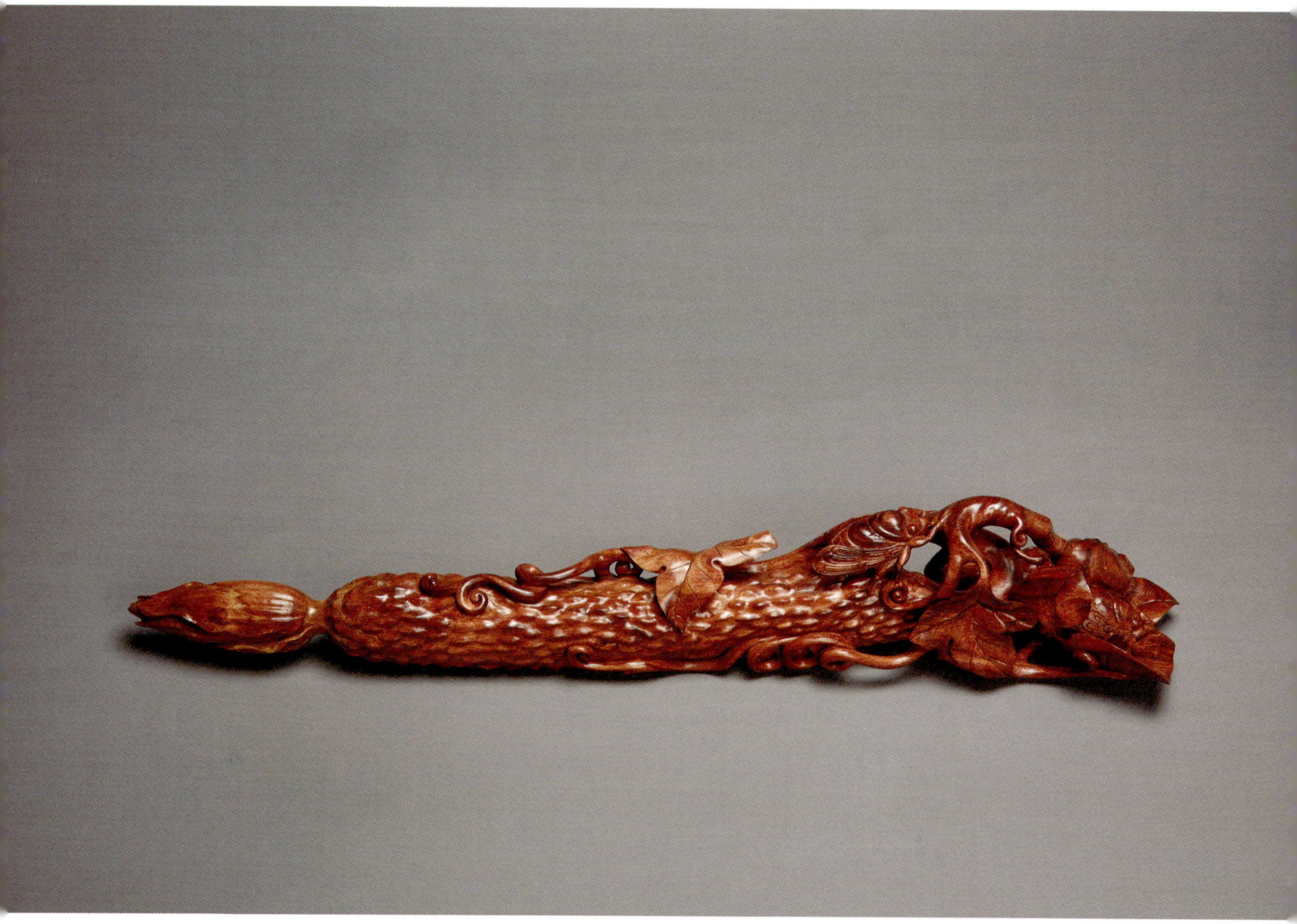

苦尽甘来

长：40.5厘米　宽：9厘米　高：7.8厘米　重：290.5克　款：三才

竹枝歌（其五）

明 • 刘基

荣华未必是荣华，园里甜瓜生苦瓜。
记得水边枯楠树，也曾发叶吐鲜花。

几年前一个偶然的机会，我从仙游一位朋友处得到这块越黄干料，其密度一般，油性尚佳，香气不甚明显，属中性料，不太受原主人重视，随意雕成一支火炬小样便束之高阁，后流落于我手。因其体积较大，年代不久但也绝非新料，经匠人改刀，使之脱胎换骨。这便是这件《苦尽甘来》的由来。

作品主体是苦瓜和蝉，寓意苦尽甘来，一鸣惊人。油性一般的越黄干料，经精细打磨后，亦能神采焕发，同时表面标准糠梨镂空之后，里面的纹理纤毫毕现、丰满有力，可谓将这款料的潜力发掘到了极致。这款作品的呈现过程配合着其主题寓意，无论是对于伏案苦读的学子，还是天涯奔波的商人，都是十分美好的心理寄托。

苦瓜本身又称"君子菜"，因其自身虽苦，却不会让同炒的其他菜混入苦味。其别名叫"锦荔枝"，为葫芦科植物，原产于印度，古称"南番"，明末才传入我国。《本草纲目》有载："苦瓜原出南番，今闽、广皆种之。五月下子生苗，引蔓茎，叶卷，须并如葡萄，而小，七、八月开小黄花，五瓣如碗形，结瓜长者四五寸，短者二三寸。青色，皮上痱谷如癞。"又《广阳杂记》记载："苦瓜，即北方之癞葡萄，江南之锦荔枝也，闽、广、滇、黔人皆喜食，味甚苦，非虚寒所宜也。"苦瓜藤相互缠绕，绵绵延延，寓意着子孙后代有福，前人的余荫庇佑着子孙后代，忆"苦"思"甜"，还可以解释成爱情甜甜蜜蜜、缠缠绵绵。明人刘基（字伯温）有苦瓜诗一首，其中"荣华未必是荣华，园里甜瓜生苦瓜"一联为古今咏苦瓜最有名的句子，表达了一代圣贤辩证达观的人生态度。

苦尽甘来
（局部）

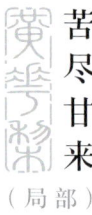

Where Bitterness Ends, Sweetness Begins

Length: 40.5 cm   Width: 9 cm   Height: 7.8 cm   Weight: 290.5 g   Sculptor: San Cai

Bitter Melon（5）
By Liu Ji of the Ming Dynasty

Wealth and fame cannot always be,
As if bitter melons may hide in a garden where sweet melons grow.
Even a withered Phoebe zhennan by the waterside can sometimes sprout.

I had a chance a few years ago to obtain this piece of Vietnamese scented rosewood from a friend in Xianyou County in Putian, Fujian Province. Its density is ordinary while its oiliness is good. Its fragrance is not very obvious. It is of a neutral material. It wasn't highly valued by the original owner. It was carved into a little torch and then left on the shelf somewhere. It found its way into my hands. Its volume is rather large and even though it has a history of only a decade or so, it is absolutely not new. The piece was re-sculpted by a friend, we adjusted its head and changed the body. This is the origin of the "Where Bitterness Ends, Sweetness Begins" item.

The main part of the work is the bitter melon and the cicada. It symbolizes "Where bitterness ends, sweetness begins, amazing the world with a brilliant feat." The Vietnamese scented rosewood has an ordinary oiliness. After it was finely polished, it shines expressively. At the same time, after the surface of the standard, dry scented rosewood was hollowed out, the vein lines were completely revealed, well developed, and vigorous. It can be said that the potential excavated from this section of material reached its peak. It conforms to the theme of "Where bitterness ends, sweetness begins, amazing the world with a brilliant feat." Whether you're a student bending over a desk studying hard or a businessman rushing to all over the world, the theme brings an absolutely beautiful hope to mind.

Bitter melon is also called "a nobleman's dish", because even though it is bitter, its bitterness won't affect other cooked dishes. It is also called "jin li zhi". It is a bottle gourd plant, originally grown in India. In ancient times it was called "nan fan". It was imported into China in the end of the Ming Dynasty. *Compendium of Medical Herbs* writes, "Bitter melon comes from Nan Fan, which is modern Fujian, Guangdong, and Guangxi provinces. All species sprout towards the end of May. It grows stalks and curled leaves. They must be together like grapes. In July and August, little yellow flowers bloom. They have five petals like a bowl. Bigger melons are about four to five inches long; the smaller ones are about two to three inches. It's blue-green and the skin is bumpy like scabies." And *Various Records of Guangyang District* writes, "Bitter melons are scabies grapes of the north and 'jin li zhi' of regions south of the Yongtze River. People of Fujian, Guangdong, Guangxi, Yunnan, and Guizhou are all fond of this vegetable. The taste is extremely bitter. They're suitable for those not deficient of 'cold'." Bitter melon vines twist around each other, extending continuously, which implies future generations are blessed and the predecessor's surplus blesses their descendants. In remembering the "bitter", you think of the "sweet". You could also explain it as love being very sweet and touching. Liu Bowen of the Ming Dynasty wrote a poem about bitter melons. "Wealth and fame cannot always be, as if bitter melons may hide in a garden where sweet melons grow", this antithetical couplet is the most famous line praising bitter melons both then and now, and shows the philosophy of life of the sage of that generation.

莲蛙

莲 蛙

长：48厘米　宽：5厘米　高：10.5厘米　重：368.6克　款：九品

约客
宋·赵师秀

黄梅时节家家雨，青草池塘处处蛙。
有约不来过夜半，闲敲棋子落灯花。

数年前我曾从一位朋友处得到一段带枝丫的越南黄花梨老料，其颜色暗红，油性上佳，缺陷是棕眼略粗，纹理较乱，算是开门的越黄北方料，闲置家里多年无人问津。去年，从柜底翻找出后，托付任兄请九品雕刻，最终成器为这件莲蛙。

作品本身以六节藕为主体，上面辅雕以两叶开荷，一叶卷荷，一只莲蓬，一朵荷苞和两只青蛙。整体随物赋形，在最大限度利用原材的同时，布局步步精妙，施以非凡人工，最终成型大方精巧、笔力精湛，实为一件珍品。

荷叶、荷花、青蛙、莲藕在中国传统文化中均寓意着吉祥，本件作品集齐了这四种元素，可谓并蒂花开，多喜临门。莲藕和青蛙都是多子的，"蛙"谐音娃娃的"娃"，祈求多子多孙、繁衍子嗣，"莲"又谐音"连"，因此二者结合寓意"连生娃娃"。同时莲花象征着美好圣洁，佛教中各路菩萨或端坐莲花宝座，或手执莲花，或作莲花手势，或作向人间抛洒莲花状。

以谐音作为对美好事物的期望，仅仅是最浅显的寓意。在中国传统民俗文化中，相比于莲花，青蛙的寓意要深刻得多。首先，青蛙的两对大眼睛分布于身体两旁，可以看清周遭的一切；其次，青蛙的叫声清脆响亮，通达四方，因此，青蛙有"四通八达，呱呱来财"的寓意。另外，青蛙单次排卵就可达数千枚，因此在古代常作为生殖崇拜的对象。辛弃疾词曰"稻花香里说丰年，听取蛙声一片"。青蛙是有益的动物，能除害虫，保护庄稼，是庄稼得以丰收的大功臣，所以青蛙同时亦蕴含有丰收的寓意。

莲 蛙
（局部）

Frogs on Lotus

Length: 48 cm   Width: 5 cm   Height: 10.5 cm   Weight: 368.6 g   Sculptor: Jiu Pin

Inviting Guests
By Zhao Shixiu of the Song Dynasty

During plum season,
Households are overtaken in rain and grass and ponds are covered in frogs.
Friends are invited to spend half the night,
Idly playing chess underneath flower-like light.

Several years ago, I received an aged branch of Vietnamese scented rosewood from a friend. Its color was dark red and its oiliness was outstanding. Its defect was that its brown flecks were slightly coarse and the wood grain was a bit disorderly. It was a real northern Vietnamese scented rosewood. It was left unused in my home for many years. Having discovered it in the bottom of a cupboard, it was given to Mr.Ren to help ask for a carving by Jiu Pin. The final product was turned into this "Frogs on Lotus".

The item uses six sections of a lotus root as the body. Complimenting the carving are two open lotus leaves on top, a curled lotus leaf, a lotus seed head, a lotus flower bud, and two frogs. The entire object follows its natural form, using the material to its highest degree and at the same time arranging everything exquisitely. Extraordinary workmanship was carried out and ultimately formed a valuable object with a shape that is natural, elaborate, and its style exquisite.

Lotus leaves, lotus flowers, lotus roots, and frogs in Chinese traditional culture all symbolize good luck. This piece pairs these four elements together nicely, bringing more joy to one's house. The lotus root and frogs both have many offspring: "frog" ("wa") and "baby" (also "wa") are homonyms, symbolizing many descendants or heirs. "Lotus" ("lian") and "continuous" (also "lian") are homonyms. As such, the two together symbolize "continuously having offspring". At the same time, lotus flowers symbolize beauty and purity. Bodhisattva in Buddhism have images of sitting upright on a lotus flower like a throne, grasping a lotus flower in hands, having a lotus - like gesture, or having the posture of throwing lotus to the world.

Homonyms are merely used as the most obvious message to express the expectation of beauty. In traditional Chinese culture, the meaning behind frogs is much more profound compared to lotus flowers. First, the two big eyes of a frog are on the sides of the body. It can see clearly its surroundings. Secondly, a frog's sound is loud and clear, being understood clearly from all directions. As such, frogs symbolize "roads extend in all directions, and their sound bringing wealth". In addition, frogs need only ovulate once to produce thousands of eggs. Therefore, in ancient times, they were often worshipped as an object of reproduction. As Xin Qiji wrote, "It will be a prosperous year, because a frog croaked from among the flowers and the paddies." The frog is a profitable animal. They get rid of insects and protect crops, contributing greatly to bumper harvests. So, at the same time, frogs also symbolize bumper harvests.

灵猴捞月

灵猴捞月

长：8厘米　宽：5厘米　高：23.5厘米　重：183.8克　款：九品

达观禅师昙颖住隐静兰若或言自此猕猴散走不来颖尝晒
日吾知是山枇杷为多始至也未实故其去将实也必群集后
果然颖恶乎俗之好异恐传以为人惑欲予咏而播之

宋·梅尧臣

隐静山中寺，猕猴往往过。
导师归以去，卢橘熟还多。
禅地宁求稀，居人切莫讹。
未尝嫌此物，任挂古松柯。

这件《灵猴捞月》作品最夺人眼目的地方是它的题材，这个故事在中国可谓家喻户晓，世人多以欢乐的传说给小孩当童话讲。其实它有更深层的含义：灵猴捞月，不知月本在天上，可隐喻为人生如梦幻泡影，如电复如露，印合了禅宗的人生。本件作品由四部分构成，分别是一轮明月、一池春水、一棵老树、三只灵猴。

据《法苑珠林》卷五十三引《摩诃僧祇律》记载："佛告诸比丘：过去世时，有城名波罗奈，国名伽尸。于空闲处，有五百猕猴游行林中，到一尼俱律树。树下有井，井中有月影现。时猕猴主见是月影，语诸伴言：'月今日死，落于井中，当共出之，莫令世间长夜暗冥。'共作议言：'云何能出？'时猕猴主言：'我知出法。我捉树枝，汝捉我尾。展转相连，乃可出之。'时诸猕猴即如主语，展转相捉。小未至水，连猕猴重。树弱枝折，一切猕猴堕井水中。"佛陀以此故事讽喻那些自以为是，分不清是非虚实，害己害人的外道邪师。

灵猴捞月（局部）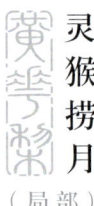

Monkey Fishing Up the Moon

Length: 8 cm   Width: 5 cm   Height: 23.5 cm   Weight: 183.8 g   Sculptor: Jiu Pin

Monkeys in the mountain
By Chang Jian of the Tang Dynasty

From the distance, the voice of the monkeys is clear and sorrowful,
Partridges are flying under the sunset.
Weeping in the lovesick mountain with the tears falling down,
The lovesick heart has been broken with the crying of monkeys.

The area that draws the eyes most in this item of "Monkey Fishing Up the Moon" is the subject matter. It can be said that this story is well-known in China. Plenty of people tell this happy legend as a children's fairy tale. Actually, it has a much deeper meaning. A monkey fished up the moon without knowing the moon was originally in the sky. It can be used as a metaphor for life being like an illusion, transient like lightning or the morning dew, suiting a Zen Buddhist life. This item is composed of four parts: the bright moon, the spring pond, an old tree, and three monkeys.

According to the introduction of Volume 53 in *Fa Yuan Zhu Lin*, "Shakyamuni told the monks, In the past, there was a city called Poronai in Jiashi Country. In the open place, 500 macaques played in the woods and then came under a Nyagrodha tree. At the bottom of a tree is a pond. In the pond, a reflection of the moon appears. A macaque sees the image of the moon and says to all his companions, 'The moon died today. It fell in the pond, We can get it out and save the world from a long dark night fall.' The other monkeys asked, 'How do we get it out?' The macaque said, 'I know how. I'll clutch a branch, and you clutch my tail. We'll form a link and get it out.' Then all the macaques did as he said and held onto each other. The tree was weak and the branch broke and all the monkeys fell in the pond." Buddha used this parable about those who believe oneself to be infallible, those who don't know right from wrong, true and false, those evil teachers hurting themselves and hurting others.

荷叶金蟾

荷叶金蟾

长：17厘米 宽：7厘米 高：5厘米 重：151.3克 款：三阳

六宫戏婴图（节选）
元·杨维桢

黄云复壁椒涂苏，银床水喷金蟾蜍。
宜男草生二月初，燕燕求友乌将雏。
芙蓉花冠金结楼，飘飘尽是瑶台侣。
宫中个个承主恩，岂复君王梦神女。

这件作品材质为一块油性出众的糠梨，雕的是一叶卷荷中卧着一只金蟾，其口衔一枚钱币，寓意财源广进、招财纳福。

在中国古代关于金蟾有一个负有盛名的传说，即"刘海戏金蟾"（本书记载了多个版本，前两个版本可参见《枯荷金蟾》《招财金蟾》）。传说，古时常德城内丝瓜井里有只金蟾，经常在夜里从井口吐出一道白光，直冲云霄，有道之人乘此白光飞升入仙。住在井旁的青年刘海，家贫如洗，为人厚道，事母至孝，经常到附近的山里砍柴，卖柴买米，与母亲相依为命。一天，山林中有只狐狸修炼成精，幻化成美丽俊俏的姑娘胡秀英，拦住刘海的归路，要求与之成亲。婚后，胡秀英欲济刘海登天，口吐一粒白珠，给刘海做饵子，垂钓于丝瓜井中，那金蟾咬钩而起，刘海乘势骑上蟾背，纵身一跃，羽化登仙而去。后人为纪念刘海行孝得道，在丝瓜井旁修建蟾泉寺，供奉刘海神像。

这个流传至今的神话故事寄托了中国古人对于往生与现世的追求，寓意着人们追求幸福、追求财富的心理寄托。此后，"三足金蟾"的形象逐渐被固定下来，被世人引以为，可以招财致富、镇宅辟邪的吉祥之物，后世的文玩圈内由此涌现了无数以此为据的物件、把件。

荷叶金蟾（局部）

Gold Frog on a Lotus Leaf

Length: 17 cm Width: 7 cm Height: 5 cm Weight: 151.3 g Sculptor: San Yang

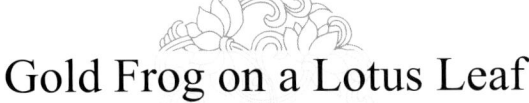

Maid Playing with Children (Excerpts)
By Yang Weizhen of the Yuan Dynasty

Decorate the wall with auspicious clouds,

And hats with spices,

a silver chair and a water-spraying gold frog are in the room.

At the beginning of February when Yinan Grass grows,

the swallows are finding mates and the crows are playing with their fledglings.

Maids of the gold palace wear hats decorated with hibiscus flowers.

They seem to be fairies from the heaven.

With the maids' company,

The emperor doesn't need to dream of the goddess.

This item's material is from a piece of dry scented rosewood with outstanding oiliness. The carving is of a gold frog lying on a curled lotus leaf, holding a coin in its mouth. The implied meaning is that you will have numerous sources of revenue, welcoming riches, and a life of ease.

In ancient China, there was a famous legend about a gold frog, "Liu Hai and the Gold Frog". The legend goes: during ancient times, there was a gold frog in Loofah Well in Changde City. At night, it would often spit out a ray of white light to the sky. A wise and just person could ride this ray of light to ascend to immortality. A young man named Liu Hai lived beside this well. He was extremely destitute, but was kind and honest and was obedient to his mother. He frequently went to the nearby mountains to chop firewood and sell it to buy rice. He and his mother relied on each other to survive. One day, in the forest of the mountains, there was a fox practicing austerities to become a spirit. It transformed into a beautiful, attractive, and intelligent girl named Hu Xiuying. It stopped Liu Hai from going back and asked him to marry her. After they were married, Hu Xiuying wanted to help Liu Hai ascend to the heavens. It spat out a white pearl and gave it to Liu Hai to use as fish bait. He fished at the Loofah Well and the gold frog bit the bait and was brought up. Liu Hai seized the opportunity and rode the frog's back. He lept with one jump, ascended, and became immortal. In order to commemorate Liu Hai's filial piety and achievement of immortality, later generations built the Frog Spring Temple next to the Loofah Well with an statue of Liu Hai.

Ancient Chinese people have been passed this myth down, hoping in the pursuit of this life and the afterlife. The meaning implies that people hope in the pursuit of happiness and wealth. Afterwards, the image of the three-legged gold frog has gradually become fixed — an object of luck to people. It can invite in wealth and ward off evil spirits. Countless people within the collector's items circle view this item this way.

天子之玺
黄华梨

天子之玺

长：5.5厘米　宽：5.5厘米　高：7.2厘米　重：131.7克　款：五谷

东川高仆射（节选）

唐·李洞

油幢影里拜清风，十里貔貅一片雄。
三印锁开霜满地，四门关定月当空。

　　这件海黄貔貅玉玺是一件印章类雕件，由一整块海南黄花梨老料雕刻而成，上部印纽雕以一只瑞兽貔貅，气韵饱满，神采标致；下部海黄纹理清晰，结构分明，丰筋多力。

　　玉玺又称"御玺"，是古时天子御用印章。秦朝时规定"玺"仅能为皇家所独称，臣民所用的章只能称为"印"，并沿用至后代。

　　"玺"作为权力与威严的象征，其上部的印钮（即"印鼻"，亦称"印首"）不仅是为了方便印章系佩于身，便于使用；亦是审美的体现、雕刻艺术和祥瑞寓意的交汇。本件玉玺，印首饰以貔貅，貔貅雄峻，黄花梨老料稳健，二者如切如磋，如琢如磨，相得益彰，堪称大师之作。

天子之玺
（局部）

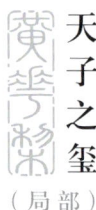

Chinese Scented Rosewood Emperor's Seal

Length: 5.5 cm Width: 5.5 cm Height: 7.2 cm Weight: 131.7 g Sculptor: Wu Gu

Gao Puye in Dongchuan（Excerpts）
By Li Dong of the Tang Dynasty.

In the shadow of oil curtain cloth I greet the refreshing breeze,

strong and intrepid troops covering ten li.

Three seals are opened by the lock, and the frost covers the ground,

Four doors are closed, and the moon hangs high in the sky.

This Chinese scented rosewood Pi Xiu (a mythical animal that brings luck and wards off evil) seal was made from an entire piece of aged Chinese scented rosewood. The top portion features a carving of an auspicious Pi Xiu full of character and beautiful expression. The lines of the wood grain in the bottom portion are distinct, the structure is clear, and the appearance is powerful.

Seal, "玉玺" ("yu xi"; literally "jade seal"), is also written "御玺" (also "yu xi"; meaning "emperor's seal"). It was the seal used specifically by the emperor in ancient times. During the Qin Dynasty(221B.C.–207B.C.), "xi" (玺 ; seal) was set to be used only by the emperor. Seals used by ordinary people were called "yin" (印), which continues to be used in later generations.

"Xi" was regarded as a symbol of power and dignity. The top, knob-like portion of the seal, "yin niu", also called "yin bi", was not only attached to the top of the seal for convenience and ease of use, but it was also a combination of a reflection of esthetics, a kind of art and meaning of luck. This Chinese scented rosewood seal is adorned with a Pi Xiu. Pi Xiu is mighty and lofty and the aged scented rosewood is firm. Both are cut and polished, complimenting each other. It is a work done by a master craftsman.

金玉满堂

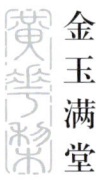

金玉满堂

长：57厘米　宽：24厘米　高：10厘米　重：1750克　款：九品

江南

<small>汉乐府</small>

江南可采莲。莲叶何田田，鱼戏莲叶间。
鱼戏莲叶东，鱼戏莲叶西。
鱼戏莲叶南，鱼戏莲叶北。

这件越南黄花梨紫油梨摆件是我所有藏品中最为钟爱的，其料质本身为一块极出色的越南北方紫油梨老料，质地细腻，色蕴深沉，棕眼全无，降香迷人，见过的朋友无不为之倾倒，实乃越北料中的极品。

整件作品的主体为金鱼嬉戏于一片荷塘之中，由此得名《金玉满堂》。最惊艳的为那四尾金鱼，其身金鳞片片，纤毫毕现，头顶的绣球与身后的尾巴均生动非常，其间最富神采的一尾金鱼，悠游荷丛之中，水波荡开，嘴角留下了一小串仙沫。两只趴于荷叶上的青蛙也神采非凡，一只双腿蹬地，静如处子，呈扑食状，另一只泰然自得，仿若晒着日光浴。

荷花、莲蓬、金鱼、青蛙这四个要素在中国传统文化中寓意吉祥。莲蓬和青蛙的寓意，主要是多子。莲蓬本多子，莲子又有"连子"寓意，莲藕谐音"连偶"，而且莲藕根茎繁密，繁殖力强。传统图案中的"鱼戏莲""鱼穿莲"，又有男女交合的隐喻。山西人民从"鱼穿莲，十七十八儿女全""鱼儿戏莲花，夫妻结下好缘法"等民间俗语，衍生出了祈求人丁兴旺的吉祥寓意，所以在和婚俗有关的器物上，往往也刻绘着各种莲花图案。青蛙的"蛙"谐音娃娃的"娃"，所以翡翠青蛙寓意贵子临门、子孙满堂，寄托了人们祈求多子多孙、儿孙满堂的美好愿望。除了多子，青蛙还因其声若鼓钟，被人们寄托了四通八达、八面玲珑的意思，商界尤重。

鱼和荷花的组合主要是谐音"连（莲）年有余（鱼）"，通常由鲤鱼和莲花组成。莲花是中国传统吉祥意象的重要代表，它广泛存在于佛教八吉祥图纹、道教暗八仙图纹和民间吉祥图案中，寓意吉祥、高洁、多子多福，有着深广的民俗审美文化意蕴。在中国，莲花被崇为君子，从古至今都被世人所重，被视为洁身自好、不同流合污的高尚品德的象征，古人有"莲生淤泥中，不与泥同调"之赞。而金鱼与荷花的寓意则侧重"金玉满堂"，金鱼谐音为"金玉"，寄托了对生活美好、财富满足的愿望；同时，中国古代常以"金"喻女孩，以"玉"喻男孩，"金玉满堂"还有儿女满堂、子嗣丰盈之意。

Gold and Jade Fill the Hall

Length: 57 cm   Width: 24 cm   Height: 10 cm   Weight: 1,750 g   Sculptor: Jiu Pin

Jiangnan
By Yuefu of the Han Dynasty

Lotus can be picked in Jiangnan.
Lotus leaves floating, crowded, fluttering.
Fish play between the lotus leaves.
Fish play east of the lotus leaves.
Fish play west of the lotus leaves.
Fish play south of the lotus leaves.
Fish play north of the lotus leaves.

Of all my collected works, this Vietnamese purple oil scented rosewood piece is the most treasured. The material is extremely remarkable. Its quality is exquisite, and its color is deep. There are no flecks, and its fragrance is fascinating. Everyone that saw the piece admired it greatly. It truly is the best quality of northern Vietnam.

The main part of this piece depicts goldfish playing in a lotus pond, hence it is named "Gold and Jade Fill the Hall". One of the most stunning parts of this piece is those four goldfish. The fish scales are detailed. The head embroidered with spheres and the tail are extraordinarily vivid. The fish with the most expression swims between the cluster of lotus, waves rippling out, the corner of its mouth leaving behind a string of bubbles. The expression of the two frogs lying on top of the lotus leaves are also extraordinary. One frog treads lightly across the lotus while the other is calm and content, as if sunbathing.

Lotus, lotus seed heads, goldfish, and frogs — these four essential objects in traditional Chinese culture all signify luck. The lotus seed head and frogs mainly symbolize many offspring. The lotus seed head has many seeds. Lotus seed ("lian zi") also means "continuous offspring", and lotus root ("lian'ou") and "successive chance". Their root stolon are also numerous and close together, having a high reproduction ability. The traditional images of "fish playing with lotus" and "fish passing through lotus" are also a metaphor for man and woman meeting together. People from Shaanxi, pray for the luck of having a thriving family population from such old sayings like "fish passing through lotus, seventeen or eighteen children altogether", "fish playing with lotus flowers, a way for husband and wife to tie down a good fate". Therefore, objects related to marriage customs are often engraved with various kinds of lotus flower designs. The "wa" in "qing wa" (meaning "frog") and "wa wa" (meaning "baby") are homonyms. As such, a jadeite frog symbolizes a noble son coming home or a hall filled with offspring. It gives people the beautiful desire to pray for many descendents, enough descendents to fill the hall. Aside from many offspring, due to a frog's voice sounding like drums, people take it to mean roads being open from all sides or everything going smoothly, especially in the business world.

The combination of lotus and fish is mainly for their homonyms: "continuously ('lian') having abundance ('yu'; also meaning 'fish')". Usually the image is composed of carp and lotus flowers. Lotus flowers are an important representation of luck in Chinese tradition. They exist extensively in the eight auspicious treasures of Buddhism, the eight immortals of Taoism, and people's idea of luck. They are a sign of luck, noble and clean-living, many offspring, and have a deep and wide inner meaning in popular customs and esthetic culture. In China, lotus flowers are esteemed as having noble characters and have had a reputation since ancient times until today. They are seen as a symbol of clean-living and honesty, and of one's noble, moral character being washed clean. People of ancient times hereby praised it by saying, "lotus grew in the sludge, but is not in agreement with the mud."

The meaning of goldfish and lotus places particular emphasis on "gold and jade filling the hall". "Goldfish" ("jin yu") and "gold and jade" (also "jin yu") are homonyms. It gives people a desire for a beautiful life and satisfying wealth. At the same time, during ancient times, "gold" was often a metaphor for a girl and "jade" was a metaphor for a boy. "Gold and jade filling the hall" also has a meaning of offspring filling the hall and well-rounded heirs.

如意灵芝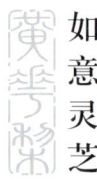

如意灵芝

长：13.5厘米　宽：7厘米　高：2厘米　重：32.5克　款：立人

早发灵芝望九华寄杜员外使君
唐·曹汾

戴月早辞三秀馆，迟明初识九华峰。
嵯嵯玉剑寒铠利，袅袅青莲翠叶重。
奇状却疑人画出，岚光如为客添浓。
行春若到五溪上，此处褰帷正面逢。

儒家把灵芝菌盖上的一轮轮云状环形纹视作祥瑞的代表，称其"瑞片"或"庆云"，古人常用的玉如意的头部也常为庆云图，寓意吉祥如意。班固《灵芝歌》中说："因灵寝兮产灵芝，象三德兮瑞应图。延寿命兮光此都，配上帝兮象太微，参日月兮扬光辉。"其本身是祭祀的歌，可见古代的皇室常以灵芝代表君主万寿无疆，名流之士门前亦常挂灵芝，以寓意吉祥如意、福祚绵延。

同时神话传说中亦不乏灵芝的身影，麻姑给西母娘娘祝寿所献的寿礼，便是用灵芝酿造的美酒。传奇野史中则常常将灵芝视为起死回生、延年益寿的仙药，《列子·汤问》曰："煮百沸其味清芳，饮之目明、脑清、心静、肾坚，乃宝物也。"而佛教自印度传入中国后，古人按照当时的心愿，让佛手持灵芝如意，这可以说是东西方文化交流和相互影响，可见灵芝在古人的思想中一直寄托着相当高邈的寓意。

如意灵芝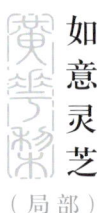
（局部）

Lingzhi Mushroom of Satisfaction

Length: 13.5 cm   Width: 7 cm   Height: 2 cm   Weight: 32.5 g   Sculptor: Li Ren

Departing from Lingzhi Early in the Morning, Looking at Mount Jiuhua, then Writing a Poem to Official Du
By Cao Fen of the Tang Dynasty

I left Sanxiu Pavilion with the moon above my head,
And then saw Mount Jiuhua at dawn.
The precipitous mountains are like jade swords,
Enshrouded by green plants.
The outline of the mountains is so unique as if in a painting,
And the beautiful scenery touches the visitors deeply.
If you travel to Wuxi in the spring, lifting the curtain,
And all this will leap into your eyes.

The Confucian school took the round, cloud-like lines of lingzhi mushroom caps to represent an auspicious sign, calling it a "lucky disk" or a "cloud of jubilation". People of ancient times commonly made the head of the jade "ruyi" scepter into clouds of jubilation. The meaning implies luck and satisfaction. Ban Gu in *Song of the Lingzhi Mushroom* states, "Lingzhi mushrooms grow in the place where the emperor has lived, which symbolizes that the three virtues of the emperor are in response to the auspicious omens. Lingzhi mushrooms can prolong life, and the glory of their presence shines on the city. They symbolizes the Taihui Star and the light shines on the emperor like the sun and the moon." The song itself is the one that is offered to the gods. It can be seen that ancient royal families often used lingzhi mushrooms to wish for the longevity of the monarch. Celebrated scholars also often hung lingzhi mushrooms on their front door. The meaning implies luck, satisfaction, and continual happiness and blessings.

At the same time, legends don't lack the silhouette of lingzhi mushrooms. Ma Gu's (a goddess in Taoism) gift offered to the Queen Mother of the West (a goddess in Chinese mythology) was a good wine made from lingzhi mushrooms. Popular legends often view lingzhi mushrooms as a legendary herb being able to raise people from the dead and extend one's life. The Tangwen Chapter in *Lie Zi* states, "Boiling it is fragrant and clean, and drinking it makes the eyes clear. It is calming and cleanses the mind. It is a treasure." However, after Buddhism was brought to China, people from ancient times, according to their aspirations at the time, let the Buddha hold a "ruyi" in the shape of a lingzhi mushroom as a symbol of good fortune. You could say this item embodies cultural exchange influencing each other. It can be seen that the lingzhi mushroom in the mind of people from ancient times always had a high and profound meaning.

瑞芝仙草

瑞芝仙草

长：24.5 厘米　宽：7 厘米　高：2.5 厘米　重：29.2 克　款：九品

水调歌头·瑶草一何碧

宋·黄庭坚

瑶草一何碧，春入武陵溪。
溪上桃花无数，枝上有黄鹂。
我欲穿花寻路，直入白云深处，浩气展虹霓。
只恐花深里，红露湿人衣。

坐玉石，倚玉枕，拂金徽。
谪仙何处？
无人伴我白螺杯。
我为灵芝仙草，不为朱唇丹脸，长啸亦何为？
醉舞下山去，明月逐人归。

在汉朝的时候，灵芝被称为"瑞芝"或"瑞草"。当时的封建统治者希望以此表达自己所行的国事能恩泽万物、德被草木，从而得到上天的嘉许，以印证统治的合法性。汉武帝在位时，因皇宫年久失修，屋檐上长出了灵芝样的东西，后宫管后勤的官员为了推卸责任就对汉武帝说这是因为皇上功德无量，上苍赐福，长出了灵芝。汉武帝听后非常高兴，下令民间进贡灵芝，从那时就兴起了采灵芝、进贡灵芝的热潮。从秦汉至明清两千多年漫长的岁月里，灵芝在宗教艺术中的地位逐渐稳固下来，除了涌现出大量的有关灵芝的典籍、诗词、绘画、雕刻等之外，还有"八仙""麻姑献寿"等神话故事被世人经久不息地传诵。

瑞芝仙草（局部）

Auspicious Lingzhi Mushrooms

Length: 24.5 cm   Width: 7 cm   Height: 2.5 cm   Weight: 29.2 g   Sculptor: Jiu Pin

Shuidiao Getou — How Green Is the Immortal Grass
By Huang Tingjian of the Song Dynasty

How green is the immortal grass, as I drift along the streams of Wuling in the spring.
Countless peach blossoms are on the sides, and orioles are in the trees.
I want to pass through the flowers and go all the way into the white clouds,
Where my great spirit would form a rainbow.
I am just afraid that deep in the flowers,
The red dew would wet my clothes.
Sitting on the jade stone, lying on the jade pillow, plucking the gold zither,
But where is Li Po?
No one can be here drinking with me with white snail-shaped cups.
I shall compare myself to the lingzhi mushrooms and immortal grass,
Not the flowers and blossoms, so no more sighing and sorrow.
I just go down the mountain after a long drink,
Accompanied by the bright moon in the sky.

During the Han Dynasty, the lingzhi mushroom was called "rui zhi" or "rui cao" ("rui" meaning auspicious). The feudal ruler at that time hoped to express that all the national affairs he performed could benefit all living things. The grass embodied virtue, thereby obtaining heaven's favor and confirming the government's legitimacy. When Emperor Wu of the Han Dynasty was on the throne, due to the imperial palace being worn down over the years, some plants that looked like lingzhi mushrooms sprouted on the roof. In order to avoid responsibility, the officials in charge of the logistics of the chambers of imperial concubines told Emperor Wu the sprouted lingzhi mushrooms were heaven's blessing due to his boundless beneficence, which made Emperor Wu extremely happy. He ordered the people to offer lingzhi mushrooms as a tributes. From then on, plucking lingzhi mushrooms came into vogue and there was a surge of offering lingzhi mushrooms as tributes. During the more than two thousand years from the Qin and Han Dynasties to the Ming and Qing Dynasties, the position of lingzhi mushrooms within religious art gradually stablized. There was an emergence of a large amount of lingzhi mushrooms—related ancient books, verses, drawings, carvings and such art pieces. In addition, Eight Immortals, Ma Gu Offering, and such mythological stories were known by every one.

苍龙教子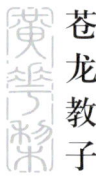

苍龙教子

长：16.5厘米　宽：9厘米　高：5厘米　重：129.9克　款：立人

老龙引子归潮图

明 • 曾烜

海门秋气横江来，怒涛殷地如奔雷。
苍龙教子习潮势，排风喷雪烟云开。
忆昔深潭事冲举，直上穹霄轻一羽。
曾嘘数滴翻瓢浆，散作九州三日雨。
只今回顾思潜踪，引子不敢施神通。
却愁幼小易飘忽，一瞬万里天无功。
我闻灵物多奇异，潜飞大小皆随意。
画师恐是张僧繇，写向生绡若真致。
龙今育子犹世人，古来有欲皆可驯。
何当重起搴龙氏，爱养留作商岩臣。

    这件立人款紫油梨作品名为《苍龙教子》，由一块质地坚硬的海黄树根料雕成。其上两条螭龙成卧状，大螭龙体态虬曲，矫健翩然，一爪踩于钱币之上；小螭龙于底部回首，形态可爱，巧稚灵朗，与大螭龙对视。母子二者做亲昵状，形神兼备，是典型的大小螭龙图。

    螭龙是传说中的瑞兽，寓意众多，在中国古代史籍中，关于它的记载和注释纷纷繁繁，莫衷一是。史载："初，汉高祖入关，得秦始皇蓝田玉玺，螭虎纽，文曰'受天之命，皇帝寿昌'。高祖佩之，后代名曰'传国玺'，与斩白蛇剑俱为乘舆所宝。"此段话经翻译可理解为：秦始皇玉玺上雕有螭虎，其后各朝纷纷仿效，常以螭为纽制作宝玺。这类史料可以表明，历史上的螭龙纹通常代表高贵和权力。

    螭龙纹兴起于春秋战国，盛于两汉，此后历代的螭龙纹基本沿袭汉代的造型。在大量出土的汉代玉器上，螭龙纹样数量众多，其中最特殊的一类是汉代玉剑璏和玉璧上的大小螭龙图。大螭龙往往占据器物的大部分空间，而小螭盘踞一隅，大小螭龙两首相对，或是大螭龙回头顾看小螭龙，抑或小螭龙回望大螭龙，表达了一种和谐相生的亲密感。

    明末清初的文人姜绍书所著《韵石斋笔谈》中记载："宋宣和御府所藏玉杯三，其一内外莹洁，绝无纤瑕，杯口耸出螭头小螭，乘云而起，夭矫如生，名'教子升天'，真神物也。二名'八面玲珑'，三则单螭作把，外多花纹，钩砑精工，莹白过于教子而神采稍逊。"这段文字明确了螭龙的教子之意，通常认为这也是苍龙教子寓意的出处。

A Blue Dragon and Its Child

Length: 16.5 cm   Width: 9 cm   Height: 5 cm   Weight: 129.9 g   Sculptor: Li Ren

Dragon Takes His Son to the Waves
By Zeng Xuan of the Ming Dynasty

The smell of autumn by the sea came face to face through the river,
And the waves rolled like thunder and lightning in the clouds.
A dragon taught his children how to control the waves.
A strong wind came and then the waves receded.
The dragon recalled that he was as light as a feather when he used
to roam the deep sea and went straight into the vast sky.
And he once bragged that he would pour down the remaining liquor
from his cup and turn it into three days of rain on the ground.
The dragon thought back to what he did, and now he follows his own child secretly
and guides the child not to mess around. But because the small dragon is petite and quick to move,
He flies away in the blink of an eye.
I have heard that strange animals are random in size when they go into the sea or fly to the sky.
I'm afraid this is painted by Zhang Sengyao. The depiction of things is lifelike like a real state.
A dragon teaches children like the human beings, to tame children since the ancient times.
This is not surprising why now some people say they want to raise dragons and take good care
of their subjects who are left as Shangyan's officials in feudal times.

This purple oil scented rosewood item, sculpted by Li Ren, is called "A Blue Dragon and Its Child. It was carved from a piece of hard Chinese scented rosewood root. The two hornless dragons are both lying down. The adult dragon's figure is curved and it looks strong and relaxed. One of its claws is clutching a coin; the small dragon is at the bottom with its head turned. Its shape is adorable. It is young and alert and looking at the adult dragon. The mother and the child are both intimately shaped, having both body and soul — it is a typical image of an adult and a child dragon.

The hornless dragon is an auspicious animal in legends. It has numerous meanings. In ancient Chinese history, records and notes are numerous and complicated and still a matter of discussion. A record states, "At first, the Emperor Gaozu of the Han Dynasty entered the Shan Hai Guan and got the Lan Tian jade seal of Emperor Qin Shihuang, engraved with the inscription, 'The emperor is under the orders of heaven.' The ancestors of the Han Dynasty immediately wore it, and it's known as the Seal of the Kingdom, served as a treasure for the emperor with the sword of killing the white snake." It can be explained that the top of Qin Shihuang's seal was a carving of a tiger dragon. Following emperors copied this one after another, often using a dragon as the knob of the seal. This historical data makes it clear that dragons in history normally represented nobility and power.

Dragons came into rise in the Spring and Autumn (770 B.C.–476 B.C.) and Warring States (475 B.C.–221 B.C.) periods. They flourished during the Han Dynasty (206 B.C.–220 A.D.). Afterwards, successive generations basically carried on the design of the Han Dynasty. There were numerous dragons within the large amount of Han Dynasty jade artifacts dug up. Among those were sword hilts and jade disks with designs of an adult and child dragon. The adult dragon often occupies the most space of the object, while the small dragon would be in the corner. Either the

adult dragon would be turning to look at the small dragon or the small dragon would be turning to look at the adult dragon, whose expressions carry a kind of harmonious, intimate feeling.
A Story of Xuanhe Jade Cup in *Yunshizhai Bitan* written by the scholar, Jiang Shaoshu of the late Ming and early Qing Dynasty, recorded, "There are three jade cups hidden in Xuanghe Yufu of the Song Dynasty. The first one's image is flexible and vigorous as if it had life. It is called 'ascended to heaven'. The second jade cup is called 'Ba Mian Linglong'. Compared with the first one, it is snow white and crystal-clear, but it is slightly inferior in expression." It was commonly believed this is the origin of the meaning of the blue dragon teaching its child.

生财有道

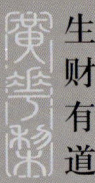

生财有道

长：7厘米　宽：7厘米　高：2厘米　重：33.2克

击蛇笏（节选）
宋·白珽

孔明庙前柏，手版贼其枝。
枯枿无生气，众目炫一时。
何如孔公笏，铁面含霜姿。
虺蛇何足道，正气屡奸欺。
祥符庆历间，岂无纤人斯。
闻之胆为落，不在彼在兹。

　　我生性怕蛇，对蛇多有抗拒，后因小儿生肖属蛇，爱屋及乌便慢慢把观念转变过来。第一次见到这件小把件时，不仅没有抗拒，心里反而甚为喜欢。小蛇体态灵动，蛇信和毒牙的刻画细致入微，加上其本身的料质相当出众，极品紫油梨的荧光令人心旷神怡，而其头顶上一圈圈纹理正好像是眼镜蛇的斑纹，虽是写意的作品，看起来却栩栩如生，活灵活现。

　　蛇在传说中是一种神物，游走于陆地、高山、江河、湖海等各处场所，古人由此常常以蛇表示事事亨通、四通八达。同时，蛇在中华民族的祖先中占有极重要的地位，在《老子》《庄子》《孟子》和《史记》等中国古代经典里，作者常常用"蛇"的概念表达深邃思想。在伏羲氏族的表象里，蛇是雷电的生命化，同时期的轩辕黄帝也曾将蛇奉为图腾，使之成为尔后道教神秘的"玄武大帝"。而西汉的杰出思想家东方朔曾对其子说，龙蛇为圣人之道。

　　在古代神话中，中国人的祖先龙脱胎于蛇，故蛇被称作"小龙"。战国时代，蛇这个循环星相学里的神兽进入了黄道十二宫，居于第六位，紧随龙之后。中国不少谚语的词源都跟"蛇"密切关联，譬如"笔走龙蛇"一语就是借"蛇"来形容中国书法点线灵活的。说到"笔走龙蛇"，就不得不提唐朝的一则典故：一天，显赫文官贺知章宴客，请怀素上人草书，李白作诗。李白对怀素上人的书法非常欣赏，便赋诗称赞其笔势如走龙蛇。

生财有道（局部）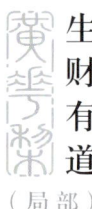

Principles Behind Making Money

Length: 7 cm　Width: 7 cm　Height: 2 cm　Weight: 33.2 g

The Hand Plate That Hits a Snake（Excerpts）
By Bai Ting of the Song Dynasty

I hit the branches of the cypress tree with my hand plate before Zhuge Liang's temple.
And all of us were enthralled by the dead branches.
But my hand plate reminds me of the one of Zhuge Liang,
Which represents his selfless and impartial appearance.
Compared with the repeated damage of villains to human integrity,
The threat of snakes is nothing at all.
In the chaos of Qingli Period of the Song Dynasty,
The most auspicious spell did not have any more effect.
All the people are afraid,
Even if not because of the chaos of the world, but the evil heart of the people.

I originally had a natural fear of snakes, feeling an opposition to them. Afterwards, because my son was born in the Year of the Snake, I slowly began to love snakes. The first time I saw this small item, not only did I not oppose it, instead, I liked it very much. The small snake is quick-witted. The snake's forked-tongue and its venomous fangs are all portrayed painstakingly down to the smallest detail. Plus, the quality of the material itself is outstanding. The fluorescence of this top-quality purple oil scented rosewood relaxes your spirit. The circle-patterned lines in the wood grain just resemble the cobra's stripes. Although the piece was done freehand, it seems quite vivid and lifelike.

Snakes in legends are a kind of mysterious creature, wandering on dry land, in the high mountains, in the rivers, in the lakes, the sea and everywhere. People from the ancient times hereby would often use snakes to express everything going smoothly and the path being open from all directions. At the same time, snakes occupied an extremely important position to Chinese ancestors. In ancient Chinese classics such as *Laozi*, *Zhuangzi*, *Mencius*, and *Records of the Historian*, the authors frequently used the concept of "snakes" to express deep thoughts. In the ideas of Fuxi Shi ethnic people, snakes were the transformation of thunder and lightning. During the same time period, the Yellow Emperor, Xuan Yuan, also made a totem of a snake, henceforth becoming the mysterious "Black Tortoise Heavenly Emperor" of Taoism. The outstanding thinker of the Western Han Dynasty, Dongfang Shuo, once said to his son, dragons and snakes are the principles of sages.

In ancient legends, ancestors of Chinese people believe snakes were born of dragons. Hence, snakes are called "little dragons". During the Warring States period, snakes, a mythological animal within astrology, was a part of the ecliptic signs of the zodiac. It ranks sixth, closely following the dragon. China has many proverbs that are closely related to snakes, such as, "Dragons and snakes follow one's brush." The word "snakes" is used to describe the nimble style of writing in Chinese caligraphy. Speaking of "dragons and snakes following one's brush", we have to mention a story from the Tang Dynasty (618–907). One day, the illustrious poet, He Zhizhang, was feasting with a guest. He asked for Huai Su the sage's cursive. Li Bai wrote poems. Li Bai very much admired Huai Su the sage's caligraphy, praising his style as being like "dragons and snakes following his brush".

松鼠佛手

松鼠佛手

长：11厘米　宽：4.5厘米　高：5厘米　重：54.7克　款：九品

咏宗良兄斋头佛手柑

明·朱多炡

春雨空花散，秋霜硕果低。
牵枝出纤素，隔叶卷柔荑。
指竖禅师悟，拳开法嗣迷。
疑将洒甘露，似欲揽伽梨。
色现黄金界，香分肉麝脐。
愿从灵运后，接引证菩提。

这件小品整体雕的是一只松鼠攀于一株佛手之上，松鼠巧稚可爱，佛手朴拙大方，这样的设计在黄花梨作品中并不多见。因黄花梨的美主要在纹理，通常雕件会留一些光面来展现黄花梨的花纹，但这件松鼠皮毛纤巧，佛手多皱，基本没有光面，因此甚为少见。

佛手因其果实成熟时状如手指得名，又叫佛手柑、五指柑、福寿柑等，据《滇南本草》记载，早在宋代我国就开始栽培佛手了。佛手花朵洁白，香气扑鼻，不仅是观赏性植物，同时也是一味极好的中药材。其花能疏肝理气，用于肝胃气滞、胸闷痰咳等症；其果除疏肝理气、和胃止痛外，还能治疗肝胃气滞、胸肋胀痛、胃脘痞满、食少呕吐等症；其根能顺气化痰，治疗肝胃气痛、脾肿大、癫痫等症。

传说很早以前，浙江金华罗店一座高山之下，住着母子两人。母年老多病，终日双手抱胸，自觉胸腹胀闷不舒，子孝，四处求医，无效。一天夜里，他梦见一位美丽姑娘，赐给他一只犹如仙女玉手样的果子，母闻后病愈。醒来后，孝子决心找到这种果子。他翻山越岭数日，筋疲力尽，某日正坐在岩石上小歇，忽听得一只青蛙叫着说："金华山上有金果，金果能救你老母，明晚子时山门口，大好时机莫错过。"孝子次日照此方法而去，只见金花遍地，金果满枝，金光耀眼，梦中姑娘飘然而来，说道："孝子感人，今送你天橘一只，可治好你母亲的病。"孝子感谢，并恳要一棵天橘苗，姑娘应允。孝子返家后，其母闻果病愈。之后他便辛勤栽培其苗，并将之传遍山村，给世人享用。后人便认为那位仙女是救世观音，天橘是观音玉手，因称之为"佛手"。

佛手的果实冬季才成熟，色泽金黄，符合中国人追求的满堂富贵的寓意，形体独特，颇堪赏玩，而其名又如指"佛祖之手"，世人认为陈设它便可避灾祸。中国自古就是信佛的，而"佛"与"福"音近，又满足了人们祈望吉祥的心理，所以佛手在中国人的心里，可以算是一种很传统的吉祥物了。

　　虽然松鼠在传统文化中的地位不是很高，但是也有一席之地，主要是象征灵活、机智、聪明伶俐。同时，松鼠经常被拆开理解，松，苍松，松柏延年，寓意长寿；鼠，是叼金钱的鼠，称为"金钱鼠"，寓意招财，所以松鼠在传统文化中通常寓意着财寿双全。

Squirrel on Buddha's Hand

Length: 11 cm　　Width: 4.5 cm　　Height: 5 cm　　Weight: 54.7 g　　Sculptor: Jiu Pin

A Poem Written to the Bergamot of the Zongliang's Table
By Zhu Duozheng of the Ming Dynasty

After the spring rain, the petals float in the air,
And the autumn frost lowers the fruit on the tree. Its branches are slender,
And the leaves roll over the fruit like the hands of a beauty.
Like the fingers raised when the Zen master grasps the formula,
The fruit is like an unfolding fist, and the successor of the Zen master is fascinated by it.
Suspicion is the hand of the Bodhisattva who will sprinkle nectar,
And seems to want to seize the cassock.
The color is as dazzling as gold,
And the aroma of pulp is similar to that of cinnamon and musk.
I hope that after Xie Lingyun, I can be led to Buddha wholeheartedly.

This small piece is a carving of a squirrel climbing atop a Buddha's Hand (also known as fingered citron). The squirrel is young and adorable. The Buddha's Hand is simple and sincere. This kind of design with scented rosewood is not common, because the main beauty of scented rosewood is in its wood grain patterns. Generally, carvings will leave plain areas behind to display the wood grain. The fur of the squirrel in this item is quite delicate, however. The Buddha's Hand has many wrinkles, almost no plain areas. As such, items like this are rare.

When the Buddha's Hand has ripened, its shape becomes like Buddha's hands, hence the name. It is also called Buddha's Hands citron, five-fingered citron, happiness and longevity citron, etc. *Herbs of Southern Yunnan* recorded that Buddha's Hands were grown as early as the Song Dynasty. Flowers of the Buddha's Hands are spotless white and aromatic. They are not a plant to just look at, however. At the same time, it is also a fabulous ingredient for medicine: its flower can relieve the liver illness. It is used for the liver, stomach, pneumothorax, coughing, etc. Aside from relieving the pain of stomach and liver, the fruit can also treat stagnation of the liver and stomach, chest aches and swelling, constipation, vomiting, etc. Its roots can transform phlegm nicely, treat liver and stomach pains, swelling in the spleen, epilepsy, etc.

Legend says long ago in Luodian in Jinhua, Zhejiang Province, a mother and her child lived at the foot of a mountain. The mother was old and had many illnesses. All day long she held her hands to her chest. She was constantly in discomfort with chest and stomach illnesses. Her son was obedient and he searched everywhere for a treatment, but to no avail. One night, he dreamt about a beautiful girl. She gave him a fruit similar to a fairy's lily-white hands. After his mom ate it, she recovered. After he awoke, the filial son was

determined to find this fruit. He spent days passing over mountain ridges. He sat on a rock one day to rest when suddenly he heard a frog said to him, "There is gold fruit on top of Jinhua Mountain. It can save your mother. Tomorrow at midnight, a gate opens on the mountain. Do not miss this opportunity." The next day, the filial son did as it had said. He saw gold flowers everywhere and tree branches full of gold dazzling fruit. The girl from his dreams floated from the air down to him and said, "The filial son is quite touching. I'll give you a heavenly citron. It can cure your mother of her illness." The filial son expressed his thanks, earnestly asked for a fruit, and the girl gave it to him. After he returned home, his mother ate the fruit and recovered. Afterwards, he worked hard to cultivate the fields, spreading the fields throughout the mountain village and letting people enjoy it. Afterwards, people believed the fairy was the goddess, Avalokitesvara, and the heavenly citron was her lily-white hands. They were called "Buddha's Hands".

The fruit, Buddha's Hands, ripen during the winter, its color and luster are golden yellow. It is in accordance with Chinese people's pursuit of riches and honor. Its figure is unique, and very delightful. Its name is literally "the hands of Buddha". People of the ancient times believed in Buddhism and believed they could avoid disasters by having it displayed. In addition, "Buddha" ("fo") sounds similar to "happiness" ("fu"). It again satisfies people's hope for luck. As such, in the heart of Chinese people, the Buddha's Hands can be considered a traditional auspicious object. Although the squirrel's position in traditional culture isn't very high, it does have its place. Its main symbol is that of agility, intelligence, and quick-wittedness. At the same time, if the word for squirrel ("song shu") is dissected: song (meaning "pine"), cang song ("cyan pine"), pine and cypress prolong life, meaning longevity; "shu" (meaning "rat"), also called money rat, is a rat that holds money in its mouth, meaning it invites riches. Therefore, squirrels in traditional culture usually symbolize wealth and longevity.

母子金蟾

母子金蟾

长：7.5厘米　宽：5厘米　高：4厘米　重：51.5克　款：天工

黑河秋雨引赋赵王孙家琵琶盖其名也
明·高启

胡天夜裂天垂泣，云压鹰低翻翅湿。
髯王醉影抱寒惊，毡殿嘈嘈箭鸣急。
红冰泪落衰灯下，倒卷河流入弦泻。
瘦驼卧碛歇铃车，扑朔阴沙鬼行野。
汉魂私语鬅风凄，都护营荒咽冻鼙。
兰山木叶连愁起，散入塞门三万里。
梦断金蟾隔烟小，青冢埋声秋不晓。

这件作品对我意义非凡，是我黄花梨入门的第一件作品，其主题是母子金蟾，金蟾体型小巧，二者共卧于一块钱币之上，空间构置精妙。大小金蟾相互呼应，精细动人，神采逼人。原本其系有挂绳，可作为挂件，但我甚为珍惜，常常握于手中把玩，从未系挂过。

"刘海戏金蟾"的民间传说版本很多，这里再介绍几个。根据《列仙全传》记载：刘玄英，号海蟾，初名操，事刘守光为相。一日忽有道人来谒，索鸡卵十枚，金钱十文，以一文置之几上，累十卵于钱若浮图（塔）之状。海蟾惊异之，曰："危哉！"道人曰："人居荣禄之场，履忧患之地，其危殆甚于此。"海蟾繇此大悟，遁迹于终南山下，丹成，尸解，有白气自顶门出，化为鹤，飞冲天。而清朝褚人获《坚瓠五集》亦载有："海蟾姓刘名喜，渤海人，十六登甲科，仕金，五十至相位。朝退，有二异人坐道旁，延人谈修真之术。二人默然，但索金钱一文，鸡卵十枚，掷于案，以鸡卵累金钱上，喜旁视曰：'危哉。'二人曰：'君身尤危何营此卵？'喜遂悟纳印，入终南山学道而仙。"

这两个故事细微处虽有出入，但是暗含的蕴意相同，即刘海蟾身居官场，但是不解官场安危，后得高人指点，大彻大悟，遂求道升仙。世人对"刘海戏金蟾"的追忆，寄托着古往今来世间人对美好未来的希冀和愿景。

母子金蟾
（局部）

Mother and Child Gold Frog

Length: 7.5 cm   Width: 5 cm   Height: 4 cm   Weight: 51.5 g   Model: Tian Gong

Autumn Rain in the Black River Area (Inspired by Lute of the Zhao Family)
By Gao Qi of the Ming Dynasty

Thunder broke up the dark sky and rain dropped consistently like tears.
Under the heavy dark clouds were eagles whose wings were rendered wet.
A drunken local man staggered down the road.
There was a noise outside the great hall where arrows rang.
Blood and tears dropped with dim light. The river is churning from the bottom up.
The emaciated camel rested on the hill, and the bells of the carriage stopped ringing.
The desert was shady and scary, as if countless wild ghosts were moving in the dark.
Han soldiers talked in the strong wind. Few people stayed in the stationed camp where the air was frozen.
The autumn leaves of Mount Lan flew around with sorrow, all over the border areas.
When I woke up, I saw the moon looming over the smoke.
The tomb was stuck in silence, not knowing that autumn had come.

The meaning behind this item is special to me. It was my introduction to scented rosewood. Its theme is a picture of a mother and a child gold frog. The bodies of the gold frogs are delicate. The use of space between the two is exquisite. They are lying on top of a coin. The adult and small gold frogs echo each other — it's meticulous, touching, and impressionable. Originally, the piece included a rope to hang it with, but I treasured it very much, often holding and fiddling with it in my hands and never hanging it anywhere.

The Complete Biography of the Immortals writes, "Liu Xuanying, one of the five northern ancestors of the Taoist Quanzhen School and God of wealth worshiped by Han folk, was referred to as Hai Chan and firstly named Cao. He was a deputy of Liu Shouguang, lord of the Five Dynasties, and was promoted to the rank of prime minister. One day, a Taoist monk came to visit him, asking for ten eggs and ten coins, and then put a coin on the table with ten eggs on it, piling them into a 'tower'. Hai Chan was very surprised and said, 'How dangerous!' The Taoist said, 'People stuck in vanity fair and precarious situations faced greater risks than this.' Suddenly Hai Chan was awakened to the truth. Since then, he retreated into Mount Zhongnan for practice. By the time the elixir was formed, his body rotted with white gas coming out of his head. Eventually he turned into a white crane and flew to the sky." Chu Renhuo of the Qing Dynasty in *Five Collections of Tough Gourd* also writes, "Liu Zhe, known as Hai Chan, born in Bohai, excelled in the imperial civil service examination at age of 16 and was promoted to prime minister at 50 years old. Having withdrawn after having an audience with the emperor, he saw two odd men sat along the aisle, talking about the practice of cultivating elixirs. They fell into silence, asking for ten eggs and ten coins, and then put a coin on the table with ten eggs on it, piling them into a 'tower'. Hai Chan was very surprised and said, 'How dangerous!' The Taoist said, 'People stuck in vanity fair and precarious situations faced greater risks than this.' Suddenly Hai Chan was awakened to the truth. Since then, he retreated into Mount Zhongnan for practice and ended up as an immortal."

Although these two stories are inconsistent in some tiny places, namely the place Liu Hai secured a position in the government; however, the implied meaning is identical. The safety and danger of officialdom was not understood, but afterwards, an able person pointed out how to achieve enlightenment and he safely sought the road to immortality. As everyone recalls, it gives people, both then and now, a hope and vision for a beautiful future.

湍濑玄芝

湍濑玄芝

长：13.5厘米　宽：7厘米　高：2.5厘米　重：56.3克　款：立人

逍遥咏
宋·赵光义

灵芝出见少人知，此是含玄故不疑。
隐逸大同非妄想，精诚自化岂参差。
翱翔碧落乘云驾，宛转虹霓入室时。
至道就中升降等，丹田日用有盈亏。

这件灵芝作品最大的特点是浅格较多，黄花梨只有中间颜色较深的"格"才是真正有用的，周围浅色的白皮毫无用处，但是白皮和格之间需要漫长的时间慢慢转换。时间越久，中间的"格"越粗，而这些格就是白皮转化而来的。可是经常有黄花梨有一些非常浅的部分，那到底是"格"还是白皮？我个人认为，这要通过考察木头的质地才能分辨，不能一概而论，最主要的分别是油性，白皮绝不会有任何油性，因此白皮再打磨，也绝不可能出现黄花梨那种荧光熠熠的色泽。而这件灵芝作品的白色部分经雕刻打磨后如盈盈秋水，色泽如玉，光彩照人，将海南黄花梨优美的材质特点表现得淋漓尽致，因此其必是浅格无疑。

关于灵芝最著名的描绘来自三国时期魏国的曹植，在其著名的《灵芝篇》中，他写道："灵芝生天地，朱草被洛滨。荣华相晃耀，光彩晔若神"，反映了诗人对灵芝的崇拜之情。而在其名篇《洛神赋》中，他又用"攘皓腕于神浒兮，采湍濑之玄芝。余情悦其淑美兮，心振荡而不怡。"形容洛水之畔神女采撷灵芝时悠闲的神态，表达诗人对神女的爱慕之情。在《飞龙篇》中，则写到其在云雾缭绕的泰山，遇到骑乘白鹿、手持灵芝的修炼者，并求养生之道的奇妙经历："晨游泰山，云雾窈窕，忽逢二童，颜色鲜好。乘彼白鹿，手翳芝草，我知真人，长跪问道。西登玉台，金楼复道，授我仙药，神皇所造。教我服食，还精补脑，寿同金石，永世难老。"体现了曹植本人对道和仙的无限追慕。

湍瀨玄芝
（局部）

Black Lingzhi Mushrooms of the Raging River

Length: 13.5 cm   Width: 7 cm   Height: 2.5 cm   Weigth: 56.3 g   Sculptor: Li Ren

Song of Ease
By Zhao Guangyi of the Song Dynasty

Talent, like black lingzhi mushrooms, is rare in the world, which is of no doubt.
It is not unrealistic that talent can be buried, and people are not all dedicated to self-education.
Talent is likely to achieve huge success, like eagles flying high in the sky.
However, there is also times when they go through ups and downs in officialdom,
And their spirits also rises and falls.

The biggest characteristics of this lingzhi mushroom piece is its light color. Scented rosewood is only useful when its color within the pith is relatively dark. The surrounding light color from the bark is not the least bit useful. The bark and pith need a very long time to slowly change. The more time that has passed, the more coarse inner pith will become. This pith, on the other hand, is precisely the result of the bark changing. However, some scented rosewood can often have extremely light sections. So is it the bark or pith? I myself believe this requires an inspection of the texture before we can distinguish the two. You can't lump two different things together. The most important distinction is the oiliness. The bark in no way can have any oiliness. As such, after polishing it again, it absolutely cannot have that fluorescent, glistening luster that appears in scented rosewood. After it was polished, the white portion of this lingzhi mushroom carving, on the other hand, is filled with autumn waters. The color and luster is bright like jade. It brings out the texture's graceful characteristics vividly and thoroughly. Therefore, this is undoubtedly a light pith.

The most famous description about lingzhi mushrooms comes from Cao Zijian of the Wei State during the Three Kingdoms period (220–280). In the famous *Writings on Linzhi Mushrooms*, he wrote, "Lingzhi mushrooms grow outside the Central Plains and red grass thrives by the Luo River. They glow and radiate, as if they were the transformation of immortals." It reflects the poet's great adoration of lingzhi mushrooms. In the famous piece, *Ode to the Goddess of the Luo River*, he wrote, "The Goddess of the Luo River reaches out her white hand, picking up lingzhi mushrooms by the raging river. I fall in love with the gorgeous goddess, and my heartbeat accelerates." It describe the leisure appearance of the goddess collecting lingzhi mushrooms by the river. It conveys the poet's admiration towards the goddess. He talks about Mount Tai surrounded by clouds and mist in *Writings on Wyverns*. There was someone who practiced asceticism riding a white deer and holding lingzhi mushrooms. He was seeking a fantastic way to maintain good health. "One morning, I visited Mount Tai. Deep in the mist-shrouded mountain, I met two young men, whose faces glowed with energy. They rode on white deers, holding lingzhi mushrooms in their hands. I knew they must be real immortals, so I knelt down to ask them how to become an immortal. They led me westward to a jade terrace, and preached to me on a golden tower. They also gave me an elixir, which was made by the emperor of gods. They taught me the right way to take the elixir, so that it can nourish my spirit and mind, make my life as long as gold, and bring me a never fading appearance." It reflects Cao Zhi's pursuit and admiration of Taoism and immortality.

闻香悟道

闻香悟道

长：8厘米　宽：4厘米　高：14厘米　重：196.3克　款：九品

焚香

明·高启

斜霏动远吹，暗馥留微火。
心事共成灰，窗间一翁坐。

此件作品名为《闻香悟道》，由一块海南黄花梨白沙料雕成，是我仅有的一件白沙料藏品。"白沙"指的是海南岛中南部的白沙黎族自治县，白沙料本身在黄花梨市场并不罕见，但是在文玩市场很少成为主角，原因是白沙地区土质肥沃，黄花梨成长很快，导致料质疏松，花纹比较宽大，虽有降香味，但极为寡淡，并不浓郁，同时白沙料糠梨比较多，出现油梨的概率极低。

此件作品，取材于香严童子闻香悟道的典故。在《楞严经卷·五》中，有二十五位菩萨分别讲自己修的法门，每个菩萨都不一样，其中香严童子所修是香因法门，以闻香悟道。《楞严经》中这样说道："香严童子即从座起，顶礼佛足，而白佛言：'我闻如来，教我谛观，诸有为相。我时辞佛，宴晦清斋，见诸比丘，烧沉水香，香气寂然，来入鼻中。我观此气，非木、非空、非烟、非火，去无所著，来无所从，由是意销，发明无漏。如来印我，得香严号。尘气倏灭，妙香密圆，我从香严，得阿罗汉。佛问圆通，如我所证，香严为上！'"意思是说：我听了佛陀教导要仔细观察一切有为法的现象后，就辞别佛陀，独自清心安静地修行。有一天看到比丘在点燃沉水香，香气寂然无声地进入我的鼻孔。我观照这阵阵香气，它既不是木头，也不是虚空；既不是烟，也不是火。它飘去的时候一点也不执着，它飘进我鼻孔也不知从何而来。我的意识也和沉香的香气一样，一时销亡清净，由此证得无漏的果位。佛陀印证了我的修行，赐给我"香严"的名号，尘俗意气一时消灭，自性妙香周密圆满，我说是从香气的庄严证得阿罗汉的果位，佛陀叫我报告如何圆满通达佛法，如果依我所证得的，以闻香悟道，这是最好的法门。

闻香悟道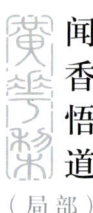
（局部）

Smelling Incense and Comprehending Taoism

Length: 8 cm　Width: 4 cm　Height: 14 cm　Weight: 196.3 g　Sculptor: Jiu Pin

Burning Incense
By Gao Qi of the Ming Dynasty

A wisp of smoke drifts away, leaving a light aroma and a spark in the incense burner.
Worries are all gone as the incense is burned into ashes — an elder sits by the window quietly.

This piece is called "Smelling Incense and Comprehending Taoism". It is carved from Chinese Baisha scented rosewood. It is the only piece I have made of Baisha material. "Baisha" refers to the Baisha Li Autonomous County in the central region of Hainan Island in the South China Sea. Baisha material itself is not at all rare in scented rosewood markets. However, few become a leading role as collectables in the marketplace. The reason is that the soil in Baisha is fertile. Scented rosewood matures very quickly, causing the material to be loose and the wood veins relatively wide. Although it is fragrant, it is not at all rich. At the same time, there are many more dry Baisha scented rosewood items. The probability of seeing oily scented rosewood is extremely rare.

The inspiration of this piece comes from the story of "Xiangyan Gets Enlightenment from Incense". In the fifth volume of *The Book of Surmounting Obstacles*, twenty-five Bodhisattva talk separately about their own pursuit of the initial approach to enlightenment. Each Bodhisattva is different. Among them, Xiangyan uses incense to comprehend Daoism. *The Book of Surmounting Obstacles* states, "Xiangyan, a disciple of Buddha once respectfully told how he got enlightenment: 'Once Buddha taught me to see all things in nature. After saying goodbye to the Buddha, I began my meditation in the quiet hall where I lived. I saw the monks burn incense, and there was a silent fragrance entering my nose. After my observation of this fragrance, I found it was neither from wood, air, smoke, nor fire, and I also found it come and go without aim. It was exactly at that moment that I got enlightenment and achieved Wulou (to be away from all worries and sorrows), and thus Buddha gave me the title Xiangyan (which means the solemn incense). Since I became Arhat, because of the incense, when Buddha asked my thoughts about the ways to get wisdom, I answered that observing the solemn incense was best!" It means: I listened to Buddha's instruction demanding that I carefully observe everything appearing as enlightenment. I at once departed Buddha, practicing Buddhism, quiet and alone. One day I saw a Buddhist monk igniting an incense stick submerged in water. The aroma slowly entered my nostrils. I looked at the waves of incense. It wasn't solid, nor was it hollow. It wasn't smoke, nor was it fire. When it floated, it couldn't be grasped. It floated in my nostrils and I didn't know where it came from. My awareness was the same as that of the fragrance of Chinese eaglewood. For a period of time, I was lost in the peacefulness. From this, I obtained mastership. Buddha confirmed my religious practice, bestowing unto me the name "Xiang Yan(solemn incense)". My worldly spirit perished. My nature was splendid and perfect. I said that it was from the aroma's dignity that gave me Arhat's mastership. Buddha called me to inform others how to understand clearly Buddhist doctrine. According to everything given to me, using the incense to understand Daoism, this is the best way to the initial approach to enlightenment.

吴牛喘月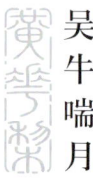

吴牛喘月

长：41厘米 宽：9厘米 高：6厘米 重：535.5克 款：三才

题竹石牧牛
宋·黄庭坚

野次小峥嵘，幽篁相倚绿。
阿童三尺箠，御此老觳觫。
石吾甚爱之，勿遣牛砺角。
牛砺角犹可，牛斗残我竹。

这件作品的材质为一块越黄老料，有赖于北京檀信的李兄帮忙，聘请了一位湘工匠人雕琢而成，落款"三才"，我给它起名为《吴牛喘月》。其描绘的是一个宁静的夏夜，荷开满塘，一头水牛和一群鲤鱼在其间悠然戏水。其写实与写意并存，在水牛的处理上尽量逼真，而在鲤鱼的雕刻上则充满浪漫与想象，是一件不凡的湘工作品。只可惜其料质一般，棕眼较粗，因此整体看来不够细腻，颇为遗憾。

传说在晋武帝时，有一个叫满奋的人，向来怕吹冷风，尤其怕寒冷刺骨的冬风。一日风大，他进宫朝见武帝，见宫内的窗户是透明琉璃所做，看起来很不坚固，不禁发起抖来，脸色变得很苍白。武帝觉得奇怪，就问他原因，满奋照实回答。武帝一听，便笑着说："琉璃窗根本是密不透风的。"满奋觉得很不好意思，便也笑着说："臣犹吴牛见月而喘。"意思是说：我就好像吴地里的牛一样，一看到了月亮就吓得喘起气来了。

满奋为什么会有这种比喻呢？那是因为我国水牛多生长在长江、淮河一带，古时称之为吴地，而牛便称作吴牛。水牛怕热，喜欢泡在凉快的水里，它只要一看到太阳，就会全身发热，喘个不停。有一次，水牛看见月亮，误以为是太阳，便吓得大大地喘起气来，"吴牛喘月"由此得名。后世人延伸其意，常用来比喻人遇事过分惧怕，而失去了判断的能力。

虽然吴牛喘月没有那么吉祥如意的象征意义，不过我却觉得用来给这件作品起名很有意境。况且牛在中华文化中是吃苦耐劳、脚踏实地、埋头苦干的典型形象，备受华夏先民的喜爱与推崇。古代文人赞牛咏牛的诗歌比比皆是，如"耕犁千亩实千箱，力尽筋疲谁复伤""长年牧牛百不忧，但恐输租卖我牛"等都表达了牛辛勤劳作、不求回报、无怨无悔的高尚品质，也传达了劳动人民对牛的尊敬、爱护之情。

吴牛喘月
（局部）

Wu Buffalo Gasping at the Moon

Length: 41 cm   Width: 9 cm   Height: 6 cm   Weight: 535.5 g   Sculptor: San Cai

A Poem of Bamboo, Stone and Cattle
By Huang Tingjian of the Song Dynasty

There is a small strange stone in the field.
At the edge of the strange stone grows tall and straight green bamboo.
There was a happy little shepherd boy riding on the back of an old ox with a three-foot whip.
I love this strange stone, little shepherd boy; please don'.t let the ox sharpen its horns on it;
But I can bear it, shepherd boy; don't let the ox fight with others or it will break the green bamboo.

This piece is made from a block of Vietnamese scented rosewood. With the help of my friend, Li, in Tanxin, Beijing, it was sculpted by an artisan and inscribed with the name "San Cai". I gave the piece the name "Wu Buffalo Gasping at the Moon". It depicts a tranquil summer night. Lotus flowers are blooming in the pond, and a buffalo and a group of carp are playing leisurely in the water. The realism and freehand style coexist. The buffalo is sculpted to be as lifelike as possible. The carp, at the same time, is sculpted to be brimming with imagination and romance. It is an extraordinary piece from Hunan. The only unfortunate thing is that the quality of the material is ordinary and flecks in the wood grain are coarse. As such, the entire work does not appear exquisite enough, which is rather regretful.

Legend says in the period of Emperor Wu of Jin, there was a person called Man Fen. He was always afraid of the cold blowing wind, especially the piercing frigid winter wind. One day the wind was quite strong. He entered into the emperor's palace to have an audience with Emperor Wu. When he saw the palace windows were made of a transparent glass, not looking very firm, he could not stop himself from shivering and his face turned pale. Emperor Wu thought it was strange. He at once asked him the reason and Man Fen replied honestly. After Emperor Wu listened, he laughed and said, "The glass windows are absolutely wrapped up tight." Man Fen felt embarrassed. He also laughed and said, "I am like a cow that saw the moon and gasped." What he means is: I am like a cow from Wu (southern Jiangsu, northern Zhejiang and Shanghai), gasping in fright the moment I see the moon.

Why did Man Fen use this kind of metaphor? Because many buffalo are grown on the Yangtze River and the Huai River region. During the ancient times, it was called Wu. The buffalo were called Wu buffalo. They were buffalo that were afraid of the heat. They were fond of soaking in the cool waters. They would only need to see the sun and at once their whole body would heat up, causing them to gasp incessantly. One time, a buffalo saw the moonlight, and mistook it for the sun, to the "Wu buffalo gasped at the moon". Later generations extended its meaning, commonly using it to describe people who are afraid to the extent they lose the ability to judge.

Although "The Wu Buffalo Gasping at the Moon" doesn't symbolize luck or good fortune, I thought this name was quite creative. Moreover, buffalo in Chinese culture are hardworking, able to endure hardships, and realistic—an image of one burying oneself in work, fully experiencing the fondness and esteem of people of the early China. The poems praised the cows can be found everywhere, such as: "Sick cattle ploughed acres of field to grow grain, tired and exhausted. Who will pity its efforts to plough?""If I've been herding cattle all year long, I don't have to worry about anything. I'm just afraid to sell it for paying the rent. All the poems express buffalo as having a noble character, being hardworking, and not seeking to go back, nor complaining. It also conveys workers' respect and love towards buffalo.

仙芝瑤草

120

仙芝瑶草

长：12厘米　宽：6厘米　高：3.5厘米　重：46.1克　款：三阳

灵芝篇（节选）
三国·曹植

灵芝生玉地，朱草被洛滨。
荣华相晃耀，光采晔若神。
古时有虞舜，父母顽且嚚。
尽孝于田垄，烝烝不违仁。

　　这款灵芝是紫油梨老料所雕，为我入门时的藏品，其主体是一柄灵芝，背面辅雕以一只口衔钱币的蝙蝠，二者互相呼应，相得益彰。

　　灵芝，世人誉为仙草，在神话传说中灵芝为仙药，服之有起死回生之功效。历代儒家、道家的渲染附会，更增加了灵芝的神秘色彩，使其成为历代帝王将相及追随者们崇拜的祥瑞物。

　　《山海经》中载有炎帝之女瑶姬不幸夭折化为瑶草的故事，比及楚国，时人宋玉在《高唐赋》中更将其夸张为人神相恋的爱情故事，其中的"巫山神女"即瑶姬。以至后人有"帝之季女，名曰瑶姬。未行而亡，封于巫山之台。精魂为草，实曰灵芝"之传说。在我国家喻户晓的神话故事《白蛇传》中，白娘子只身前往峨眉山盗取仙草救其夫许仙，所盗能"起死回生"的仙草，便是灵芝。乐府诗《长歌行》亦有关于灵芝的描绘："仙人骑白鹿，发短耳何长。导我上太华，揽芝获赤幢。来到主人门，奉药一玉箱。主人服此药，身体日康强。发白复更黑，延年寿命长。"其中说的便是灵芝延年益寿的功效。

仙芝瑤草（局部）

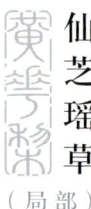

Lingzhi Mushrooms and Yao Cao

Length: 12 cm   Width: 6 cm   Height: 3.5 cm   Weight: 46.1 g   Sculptor: San Yang

Lingzhi Mushrooms (Excerpts)
By Zhi Cao of the Three Kindoms Period

Lingzhi mushrooms grow outside the Central Plain.

The red herbs by the shore north of Shaanxi are lush and blossoming.

Their brilliant light sparkles.

Yu Shun was of ancient times,

His parents were ignorant and stubborn.

He obeyed and divided the fields,

It's not against benevolence.

This piece was carved from the aged purple oil scented rosewood. It was the one that I had collected when I had first started out. The main body is the stem of a lingzhi mushroom. A bat with a coin in its mouth is carved on the back. The two correlate well, bringing out the best in each other.

Lingzhi mushrooms are praised by people for being a medicinal herb. Legend says that lingzhi mushrooms were made into potions of immortality. The Confucian and Taoist school's rendering added interpretations. They gave lingzhi mushrooms a mysterious tint, becoming an auspicious object worshiped by successive generations of regents and followers.

The Classic of Mountains and Seas recorded that the Yan Emperor's daughter, Yao Ji, unfortunately died young, turning into a medicinal herb, "Yao Cao". In comparison, Song Yu, of the state of Chu, in *Poems of Gaotang* exaggerated the story into a romance between mortal and immortal. The "Mt. Wu Goddess" was considered to be Yao Ji. Later generations told the following story:"The emperor's daughter's name was Yao Ji. She died before she could walk and was buried in Mt. Wu. Her spirit became grass called lingzhi."In the well-known mythological story in China, *Tale of the White Snake*, Lady Bai went along Mt. E'mei to take a medicinal herb to save her husband, allowing him to become immortal. What she took was actually a medicinal herb used to "raise the dead" - that is the lingzhi mushroom. Yue Fu's poem, *Chang Ge Xing*, also had a description of the lingzhi mushroom: "An immortal of long life rode a white deer. He led me to Mt. Hua to pick the red lingzhi mushroom. We came to the immortal's gate and presented a jade box of medicine. The immortal ate the medicine, his body becoming strong. The white hair turned dark again, his life being prolonged." The poem speaks of using Lingzhi mushrooms to prolong one's life.

竹节貔貅

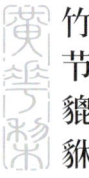

竹节貔貅

长：37厘米　宽：11厘米　高：6.5厘米　重：519克　款：天工

于潜僧绿筠轩

宋·苏轼

可使食无肉，不可居无竹。
无肉令人瘦，无竹令人俗。
人瘦尚可肥，士俗不可医。
旁人笑此言，似高还似痴。
若对此君仍大嚼，世间那有扬州鹤。

这件《竹节貔貅》是我某年在北京"而立文玩"的周年庆上拍得的，作品料质出众，威武大气，寓意吉祥，是一件不可多得的海黄紫油梨老料重器。

作品主体为一段竹节，两头相对卧着两只貔貅，口衔一串钱币，两只貔貅霸气威严、栩栩如生，竹节挺拔俊丽、细节饱满，因此题为"竹节貔貅"。整件作品料质非常细腻，几乎不见棕眼，是霸王岭一带的沉水紫油梨，为上上款。

竹在中国文化中具有深远的寓意，位列"梅兰竹菊"四君子之中，为中国美德的物质载体，乃君子的象征。中国人最早的竹情节可以追溯到魏晋时期，之后，竹从一种文化意义演变成了一种民俗的意象，其随遇而生，虚心直节，干云而上，四季常青，具有十分丰富的可延伸的寓意。同时，竹子的实用价值亦非常高，如果说北方人发明了"钻木取火"的话，那么江南人民则有"结竹成屋"的贡献。大诗人苏轼曾有诗句云："宁可食无肉，不可居无竹。"

竹节貔貅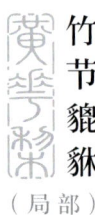
（局部）

Pi Xiu on Bamboo

Length: 37 cm   Width: 11 cm   Height: 6.5 cm   Weight: 519 g   Sculptor: Tian Gong

In Yu Qian Temple, a Monk and Bamboo Pavilion
By Su Shi of the Song Dynasty

I'd rather eat without meat,

Than reside without bamboo.

Without meat, people become thin;

Without bamboo, people become vulgar.

Thin people can become fat;

Vulgar men cannot be cured.

Others laugh at these words,

It seems lofty and foolish.

If it is right, this bamboo can still be mulled over,

And the world has a way to Yangzhou.

I acquired this piece, Pi Xiu on Bamboo, at one of the anniversary celebrations of the Beijing Er Li. The aged material of this piece is outstanding. It has a formidable atmosphere and it symbolizes luck. The purple oil scented rosewood is hard to come by.

The main body consists of a bamboo joint. Lying on both ends are two Pi Xiu (a mythological creature that brings luck and wards off evil). In their mouths are coins strung together. Both Pi Xiu are aggressive and dignified. They are vivid and lifelike; the bamboo joints are tall, straight, and beautiful. It is full of details. As such, the piece is called "Pi Xiu on Bamboo". The material of this entire work is exquisite and flecks can hardly be seen in the wood grain. It is a high grade deep purple oil scented rosewood from the Bawang mountain range.

Bamboo in Chinese culture has a profound and long-lasting meaning. It ranks within the four "nobles", that is "plum, lily magnolia, bamboo, and chrysanthemum". It is a thing of virtue and therefore a symbol of a nobleman. Bamboo can be traced back, at the earliest, to the Wei and Jin Dynasties (220–265; 265–420 respectively). Afterwards, the meaning of bamboo, from this culture, developed into an image of a kind of popular custom. It is born of luck, hollow, straight, and segmented. It soars into the sky, and remains evergreen during all four seasons. It symbolizes abundance and the ability to expand. At the same time, the practical value of bamboo is extremely high. If you were to say northerners invented the use of "wood to make fire", then people of regions south of the Yangtze River invented the use of "bamboo to make houses". The great poet, Su Shi, once wrote in a poem, "I'd rather eat without meat than reside without bamboo."

夜夜数钱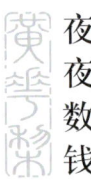

夜夜数钱

长：14.8厘米　宽：4.5厘米　高：6.5厘米　重：33克

寒夜次潘岷原韵

清·查慎行

一片西风作楚声，卧闻落叶打窗鸣。
不知十月江寒重，陡觉三更布被轻。
霜压啼乌惊月上，夜骄饥鼠阚灯明。
还家梦绕江湖阔，薄醉醒来句忽成。

这件雕件描绘的是一只老鼠趴在树叶上，取其谐音，名为《夜夜数钱》。通常情况下这样的题材一般会再加一个钱币，但是本件作品没有，想来可能是料不够，抑或只是作者练手的小品，因此没那么较真，但这并不妨碍它以鼠为财的吉祥寓意。

虽然在日常生活中，过街老鼠人人喊打，但是在中国传统文化里，老鼠很早就脱胎成了具有灵性、聪慧又神秘的小生灵，在几千年的文化传统中，其形象可谓变化万千。

从古典文学中说开来，最早记录鼠的作品是《诗经》中的《魏风·硕鼠》，而最有名的篇目则是《西游记》第八十一回写无底洞的老鼠精逼唐僧成亲。此外，志怪小说《聊斋志异》亦有《阿纤》描写人鼠恋爱，为世人所传诵；《水浒传》将绰号为"白日鼠"的白胜列为一百零八将之一；《三侠五义》中大闹东京的"五鼠"，则是为世人传诵的侠义之士。

夜夜数钱
（局部）

Counting Money Every Night

Length: 14.8 cm   Width: 4.5 cm   Height: 6.5 cm   Weight: 33 g

Staying in Panmin in a Cool Evening
By Zha Shenxing of the Qing Dynasty

The whistling of the west wind plays a musical melody in the State of Chu.
I lie in bed hearing fallen leaves pattering on the window,
Not knowing it is so chilly on the riverside in October.
At midnight I am awakened by the coldness and realize the quilt is too thin.
The heavy frost startled the crowing ravens which fly toward the moon.
Hungry rats can not stand the long night staring at the light.
Due to my homesickness I get drunk and dreamed of the broad and far river and lake,
And I write this poem as soon as I am awake.

This carving depicts a rat lying on top of a tree leaf. Considering its homonyms, it was called "Counting Money Every Night". Under normal circumstances, a coin could be added into the carving due to the subject matter. However, for this piece, it wasn't added. It can be assumed that the material was not sufficient, or the piece was merely a small work of practice for the sculptor. As such, he was not so serious. This doesn't hinder the use of a rat to mean good fortune.

Although in daily life, it is something detested by every one, in Chinese traditional culture, rats had been a spiritual nature. They are intelligent and mysterious little creatures. During thousands of years of culture, its image can be said to be ever changing.

In the classical literature, the earliest record of a rat is in *Wei Feng-A Large Rat* of *The Book of Songs*. The most famous writing is, however, in the eighty-first chapter of *Journey to the West* where it writes about the rat spirit of the Bottomless Pit forcing Xuanzang into marriage. In addition, the novel, a record of strange phenomenon, *Strange Stories from a Chinese Studio* has a story of "A'Xian", featuring love between a person and a rat, a well-known story by every one. *Water Margin* is one of the Four Classics, in which there's a character called Bai Sheng, whose nickname is Daytime Rat. In *Three Warriors and Five Righteous*, there are "five rats" that run amok in Kaifeng, but they are actually the widely known righteous soldiers.

一路连科

一路连科

长：10厘米　宽：9厘米　高：19厘米　重：94.8克　款：天工

渔歌子
<small>唐·张志和</small>

西塞山前白鹭飞。桃花流水鳜鱼肥。
青箬笠，绿蓑衣，斜风细雨不须归。

　　这件作品名为《一路连科》，是由糠梨干料所雕，原本油性不足是糠梨干料的一大缺憾，但由于本品雕的是枯莲，二者搭配相得益彰，缺陷反而成为点睛之笔，可谓化腐朽为神奇，实在是精妙之极。整件作品雕的是莲花叶茎上站立一只鹭鸟，口中叼着一条小鱼，"鹭"与"路"同音，"莲"与"连"同音，因此得名"一路连科"。旧时科举考试，连续考中谓之"连科"，寓意着士子应试成功，仕途顺利。古人甚至会把"一路连科"绣在枕头上，表示做梦都中举，实在可爱。

　　莲花相传是何仙姑的化身，其原型为一个容貌非凡的女性，手持莲花，为八仙之一。而关于八仙有一个流传很广的传说叫"八仙过海"，见于杂剧《争玉板八仙过海》。相传白云仙长邀请八仙及五圣共襄盛举，回程时八仙之一的铁拐李意犹未尽，对众仙说："都说蓬莱、方丈、瀛洲三神山景致秀丽，我等何不去游玩、观赏？"众仙激情四溢，齐声附和，这时同为八仙之一的吕洞宾说："我等既为仙人，今番渡海不得乘舟，只凭个人道法，意下如何？"众仙听了，欣然赞同，一齐弃座动身而去，聚到海边，个个亮出了自己的法宝。清婉动人的何仙姑落在后面，将莲花往海里一放，顿时红光四射，花像磨盘，仙姑亭亭玉立于莲花中间，风姿迷人，荷花托载其渡过了面前的汪洋大海。可见莲花在传统文化中便是美好和吉祥的象征。

　　另外，自古以来，鹭鸟便被世人所重视，因其羽毛洁白，姿态优美，古人常用它来象征容貌修整、品德高尚之人。如《诗经·周颂·振鹭》就用"振鹭于飞，于彼西雍"起兴，形容前来周庙助祭的杞、宋之君的美德。此外，白鹭成群飞翔时有序而不乱，史籍常以"鸿仪鹭序"来比喻文武百官在朝廷上进退井然有序的场面。到明清时期，白鹭的形象进而出现在官服上，六品文官的"补子"纹样就是白鹭。

一路连科（局部）

Journey to Continually Pass the Examinations

Length: 10 cm   Width: 9 cm   Height: 19 cm   Weight: 94.8 g   Sculptor: Tian Gong

Song of Fish
By Zhang Zhihe of the Tang Dynasty

A little egret flies in front of Xisai Mountain.

A fat mandarin fish is in the stream by the peach blossoms.

One ripple follows tens of thousands.

How does the yellow hat seem like a hat of green bamboo?

How does a sheep's wool seem like the green clothed grain? The wind-blown rain will not return.

This piece is called "Journey to Continually Pass the Examinations". It is made of dry scented rosewood. A great disadvantage of dry scented rosewood is that its oiliness is originally insufficient. However, due to the original product is sculpted into a dry lotus flower, they both bring out the best in each other. The defects instead become the shining point. It can even be said that something rotten was changed into something magical. It is really an extremely exquisite piece. The entire work is a carving of a heron hanging on the leaf of a water-lily with a small fish in its mouth. "Heron" ("lu") and "road" (also "lu") are homonyms. "Water-lily" ("lian") and "continually" (also "lian") are homonyms, as well. As such, it is called "Journey to Continually Pass the Examinations". In former times, to pass the imperial examinations continuously is called "lian ke" (literally "continually [passing] exams"). It means passing the official exams and having a good official career. People of ancient times even embroidered the phrase "journey to continually pass the exams" on their pillow. It expresses that their dream is to pass the imperial examinations, which is really lovely.

Lotuses and water-lilies in legend are the incarnation of female immortals. Their appearance is one of an extraordinary woman. One of the Eight Immortals holds a lotus in her hand. There is a legend about the Eight Immortals that has spread pretty widely called "Eight Immortals Crossing the Sea", seen in the Zaqu (a kind of musical comedy), in the Yuan Dynasty: *The Eight Immortals Cross the Sea Striving for the Jade Tablet*. The legend says the White Cloud Celestial invited the Eight Immortals and five sages to cooperate on a great undertaking. On their way back, one of the Eight Immortals, Li Tieguai, had not fully expressed himself. He said to the others, "All say Penglai Island, Fangzhang Island, and Yingzhou Island are very beautiful. Why don't we have fun and go to have a look?" The enthusiasm of the other immortals permeated the whole place. Everyone agreed in unison. At this time, one of the Eight Immortals, Lyu Dongbin said, "We are already immortals. We don't need a boat to cross the sea. How about using our own powers?" Everyone heard and gladly approved. They went on the journey simultaneously, congregating at the coast, each one revealing their own magic weapon. The clear, soft, and moving female immortal fell behind. She placed her lotus flower in the sea and immediately red light radiated all around. The flower resembled a lower millstone. The slender and elegant female immortal sat on the lotus flower—her graceful figure was enchanting. She rode it across the vast sea ahead. It can be seen that the lotus flower in the traditional culture in the ancient times was an emblem of beauty and luck.

In addition, people attached importance to the heron because its feathers were pure white and its posture was graceful. People commonly used it as an emblem to adorn one's appearance, one of noble and moral character. For example, in *The Book of Songs - Ode of Zhou - Flapping Heron*, the author starts with "A flapping heron soars, towards the west calmly", to describe one from Qi coming to the temple to help offer sacrifices and the virtue of a sage from Song. Moreover, when little egrets circle in the air in groups, they are orderly. Historical records often use "the order of large herons" as a metaphor for the clear and orderly scene of civil and military officials in the court, having a sense of propriety. During the Ming and Qing Dynasties, the officials' "emblem" pattern on their clothes was a white heron.

一鸣惊人

一鸣惊人

长：10厘米　高：6.5厘米　宽：3厘米　重：26.9克　款：九品

在狱咏蝉

唐·骆宾王

西陆蝉声唱，南冠客思侵。
那堪玄鬓影，来对白头吟。
露重飞难进，风多响易沉。
无人信高洁，谁为表予心？

　　这件虎皮纹作品雕的是一叶之上卧着两只鸣蝉，树叶纹路清晰，夏蝉小巧婉致，有着一鸣惊人的寓意。

　　古人认为蝉性高洁，《史记·屈原贾生列传》就说："蝉蜕于浊秽，以浮游尘埃之外。"认为蝉在最后脱壳成为成虫之前，一直生活在污泥浊水之中，等脱壳化为蝉时，飞到高高的树上，只饮露水，可谓出污泥而不染，故其自古以来便十分受推崇。

　　同时，蝉能入土生活，又能出土羽化。从汉代以来，皆以蝉的羽化比喻人能重生，如将玉蝉放于死者口中，成语中称作"蝉形玉含"，寓精神不死，再生复活。世人也常把蝉佩于身上，以表示高洁、不落拓世俗的精神。因此，玉蝉既是生人的佩饰，也是死者的葬玉。在汉代以来的出土文物中，我们常常可以见到各式各样的蝉形玉含，即使在现代的玉石中，也常能发现这类玉石。除了玉石，蝉纹在青铜器的装饰上也常常能见到。晋代郭璞有《蝉赞》云："虫之清洁，可贵惟蝉，潜蜕弃秽，饮露恒鲜。"以表赞蝉这种清洁和弃秽的精神。

一鸣惊人（局部）

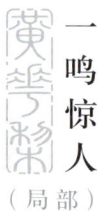

Overnight Success

Length: 10 cm   Height: 6.5 cm   Width: 3 cm   Weight: 26.9 g   Sculptor: Jiu Pin

Chanting Cicada in Prison
By Luo Binwang of the Tang Dynasty

In the autumn I heard the chirping of cicadas.
As a prisoner my deep homesickness was triggered.
While cicadas' wings were flipping vigorously,
I looked at my gray hair and felt so depressed.
Because of the heavy dew cicadas could not fly high.
Due to the soughing wind the singing quickly dissipated.
Oh, cicada, no one believes your nobleness,
And who could understand my devotion to country?

This carving of two cicadas lying on a leaf has a tiger-patterned wood grain. The veins in the tree leaves are clear and the summer cicadas are small and delicate. They symbolize overnight success.

People from the ancient times believed cicadas to be noble and clean. Records of the *Historian - The Historical Biography of Qu Yuan and Jia Yi* states, "Cicadas extricate themselves from the mud, wandering outside the dust." It was believed that cicadas, lived in muddy waters before shedding their skins and becoming an adult. When they moulted and turned into a cicada, they flew to really tall trees. They drank only dew. It could be said they come out of the mud and do not contaminate anything. Therefore, since the ancient times, they have been thought highly.

At the same time, cicadas live in the dirt and can leave the dirt after shedding their skins. Since the Han Dynasty, cicadas shedding their skins has been seen as a metaphor for people being reborn. Like placing a jade cicada in the mouth of the deceased, there is a phrase, "a cicada-shaped jade in the mouth". It implies that the spirit does not die, but is rather reborn. People also often adorn bodies with jade cicadas, using cicadas to express a noble and clean spirit, one that is not profane. Consequently, jade cicadas are both an ornament for the living and for burying the dead. Cultural relics have been dug up since the Han Dynasty. We often see all kinds of cicada shaped jades in the mouths of the deceased. Even in modern times, we can also often find these kinds of precious stones. Besides precious stones, cicada-patterns decorating bronze artifacts are also often seen. Guo Pu of the Jin Dynasty in *Cicada Praise* stated, "Of all insects, only cicadas are praiseworthy of cleanness. They break out and abandon the dirt, drink dew, and are always fresh." It praises the spirit of cicadas for their cleanness and abandoning filth.

鱼龙戏珠

鱼龙戏珠

长：21厘米　宽：7厘米　高：8.3厘米　重：137.1克　款：九品

忆秦娥·五日移舟明山下作
宋·陈与义

鱼龙舞。湘君欲下潇湘浦。
潇湘浦。兴亡离合，乱波平楚。
独无尊酒酬端午。移舟来听明山雨。
明山雨。白头孤客，洞庭怀古。

这件《鱼龙戏珠》作品是由一块海黄瘤疤料雕成，整体由八鱼一龙组成，其本身是瘤疤料，通体鬼眼鬼脸密布，加上油性出众，看起来每个鬼眼都炯炯有神、熠熠生辉。作品的正面是鱼龙驭涛驾浪，傲立潮头，活灵活现；而背面则基本没有雕刻，用一整个素面体现海黄瘤疤原生材料本身之魅力。整件作品构思巧妙，雕工精湛，可属九品的上乘之作。

海南黄花梨界有"一瘤二麻三鬼脸"的说法，说的是在海南黄花梨中最珍贵的当属瘤疤，然后是芝麻点，最后是鬼脸的花纹。"海南黄花梨瘤疤"是指黄花梨在生长过程中，由于受到外部伤害或者是自身病变产生出的木材奇特现象，也叫"瘿木"，多产自根部土壤以上空心的树干上，具体表现为木材表面长出突起的大瘤疤，并在此瘤疤上长有许多凸起如花生豆般大小的小疙瘩，成熟后的留疤料自然脱俗，不拘一格，甚至可以用鬼斧神工、天工造化来形容。

鱼龙作为中国传统文化中的圣物，在唐代时候关于它的记载最多。李白有首咏鱼龙的名作叫《赠崔侍郎》，其诗云："黄河三尺鲤，本在孟津居。点额不成龙，归来伴凡鱼。故人东海客，一见借吹嘘。风涛倘相见，更欲凌昆墟。"意思是说："三尺长的黄河鲤鱼，通常居住在孟津关一带。跳不上龙门，就点染额头，归来与凡鱼做伴。咱们是老相识了，承蒙你慧眼识珠，极力褒奖。如果今后还有风云际会的可能，希望能青云直上九重天，高居天山之巅。"

唐宋时期流行一种龙首、利齿、双翼、鲤鱼身形象的龙鱼合体纹样，是为印度传至中原的摩羯纹，摩羯是佛经故事里长鼻大口的巨鱼，进入中国后和"鱼化龙"传说相结合，成为一种颇具异域风情的纹样，因此也称"鱼龙纹"。

摩羯纹是在南北朝时期随佛教东传进入中国的，在古印度的神话传说中，摩羯身形巨大，常以兽首（鳄鱼或大象）、长鼻、大口、利齿、鱼身鱼尾的形象出现，被认为是河水之精、生命之本。《洛阳伽蓝记》记载，辛头大河（印度河）西岸有一座塔，塔身石头上是鱼鳞纹样，此处便是佛经中的摩羯国。传说中如来为了救护摩羯国中深受疮病之苦的百姓，跃入水中，化身为大鱼，摩羯国人吃了如来幻化的鱼肉，如服灵丹妙药，病体痊愈，于是摩羯鱼便成了如来的象征、佛教的圣物，受到众多信徒的顶礼膜拜。

从南北朝起至隋唐时期，伴随着佛教的传播，西来的摩羯形象经历了一个中国化的过程。在摩羯纹流传的过程中，人们渐渐为其增加了中国龙的形象特征。比如《洛神赋图》中出现的摩羯形象，卷曲上扬的长鼻子还带有印度色彩，而中晚唐之后，带角龙首、鼓目圆睁、大嘴利齿、双翼鲤鱼身的摩羯形象，已经糅合了中华鱼龙幻化的文化基因，发展为集鱼龙变化及佛教摩羯信仰于一体的复合形象，最终成为现在流行的鱼龙形象。

Dragons and Fish Playing with a Pearl

Length: 21 cm   Width: 7 cm   Height: 8.3 cm   Weight: 137.1 g   Sculptor: Jiu Pin

Yi Qin'e · Writing Aboard to Ming Mountain on May 5th
By Chen Yuyi of the Song Dynasty

Dragon-fish dance.
Qu Yuan wants to be on Xiangjiang River bank.
Xiangjiang River bank.
Rise and fall, separate and reunite, disturbed waves seen from far away.
Alone with no excellent wine to enjoy the Dragon Boats Festival.
Boating alone to hear the rain on Ming Mountain.
Ming Mountain rain. An old, lonely visitor on Dongting Lake, missing people of the ancient.

This piece "Dragon and Fish Playing with a Pearl" is made from a Chinese scented rosewood tumor. The entire piece depicts eight fish and one dragon. Its body itself is the wood tumor. The wood grain is covered densely in landscape-patterns and flecks. Plus, the wood's oiliness is outstanding. The flecks all appear glistening, bright and full of expression. The front of the carving shows a dragon and fish riding on the large waves. They stand proud in front of the tide - their image vivid and realistic. The back, however, has not been carved. It uses one complete side, void of makeup, to reflect the original charm of the Chinese scented rosewood tumor. The design of this piece is ingenious and its workmanship is exquisite. It can be categorized as Jiu Pin's best quality piece.

There is a saying in the Chinese scented rosewood circle, "One: tumor. Two: flecks. Three: landscape-patterns." It refers to Chinese scented rosewood's most precious quality: the tumor. Second are flecks. Third is wood grain landscape-patterns. "Chinese scented rosewood tumor" refers to the scented rosewood growing process, due to the exterior taking damage or experiencing pathological changes, the appearance of the wood is peculiar. This is also called "ying mu" (knob on wood). Most are produced on top of the tree trunk from above the roots in the soil, specifically displaying a large tumor sprouting from the surface of the wood. Furthermore, these tumors have many various-sized knots resembling flower sprouts protruding from the surface. After the tumor has matured, it is naturally refined, not sticking to any pattern. So much that it can be described as a supernaturally fine craft or a work of heaven.

A fish-dragon is a sacred creature in Chinese traditional culture.

During the Tang Dynasty, it was recorded mostly by Li Bai in a masterpiece about the fish-dragon called *Dedicated to assistant minister Cui*. The poem reads, "In Yellow River swam a two-foot carp, who originally lived in Meng River. He failed to jump over the Dragon Gate, coming back to keep company with common fish. They were his old acquaintances. He thanked them for their praise and admiration and for a good chance to flourish he wished he could soar to the highest top of Mount Kunlun." It means that "a carp a meter long from the Yellow River, regularly residing in a region of Mengjin, Henan. It could not leap through the dragon gate. Its forehead scarred, and it returned to accompanying ordinary fish. They knew each other for a long time and were indebted to its knowledge of the pearl and praised the fish. If there were to be another opportunity of chance, it hoped that it could rise straight up in the clear sky to nobility and stand on the top of Tian Mountain".

During the Tang and Song Dynasties (618–907 and 960–1279 respectively), a kind of creature with the head of a dragon, having sharp teeth, wings, and the body of a carp was wide spread. It was the pattern of Capricorn passed down to the Central Plain from India. Capricorn was a massive fish with a long nose and a big mouth from Buddhist texts. After it entered China, it was combined with the "fish-turned dragon" of legends. It turned into a kind of rather foreign-styled appearance. Thus, it was called dragon-fish.

The Capricorn pattern followed Buddhism being passed east into China during the Northern and Southern Dynasties (420–589). In the ancient legends of India, Capricorn's figure was huge. It was often depicted with a creature's head (an alligator or elephant), a long snout, a big mouth, sharp teeth, the body of a fish, and a fish's tail. It was believed to be a spirit of the river, the root of life. *A Record of Buddhist Temples in Luoyang* recorded that there was a pagoda on the west bank of Sindhu River (a river in India). On the stone surface of the pagoda were fish scale patterns. In addition, this is the Capricorn nation in Buddhist texts. In legends, Tathagata, in order to rescue the sick common people of the Capricorn nation, jumped into the river, his body taking the form of a fish. The people of Capricorn nation ate Tathagata's fish body. It was as if they had eaten wonder medicine—their sick bodies recovered completely. As a result, the Capricorn fish became a symbol of Tathagata, a sacred creature in Buddhism, receiving the worship of numerous believers.

From the Northern and Southern Dynasties to the Sui and Tang Dynasties, accompanying the spreading of Buddhism, the image of Capricorn from the west experienced a process of Chinese transformation. During the circulation of Capricorn, people slowly increased its Chinese dragon characteristics. For example, Capricorn's image appeared in *The Picture of The Ode of the River Goddess*. The curved, long, rising snout carries a flavor from India. However, after the mid to late Tang Dynasty, Capricorn's appearance had a horned dragon's head, round open eyes, a big mouth with sharp teeth, and wings with a body of a carp. It had already blended with the cultural genes of China's fish-dragon. It developed into a complex image of a dragon-fish and Buddhist's Capricorn, and finally turned into the popular dragon-fish figure.

知足常乐

知足常乐

长：10厘米　宽：7厘米　高：3.5厘米　重：117.1克　款：百吉

蜘蛛

宋·洪咨夔

已迫斜阳欲坠时，谋身只怕脚行迟。
纵横笼罩大为网，首尾经纶浑是丝。
腹饱飞虫肥似瓠，喙工毒螫利於锥。
朝来猛被儿童扫，不放檐牙一点遗。

知足常乐的思想源自道家，后为世人所广知，是中华传统文化中的瑰宝。文玩中经常会雕刻这个题材，最常见的表达方式就是足上雕蜘蛛，寓意知足常乐。这件作品是百吉款海黄老家具料雕手把件，作品简单大气，蜘蛛细节到位，布局精巧，令人爱不释手。"知足常乐"最早出自《道德经》第四十四章："名与身孰亲？身与货孰多？得与亡孰病？甚爱必大费；多藏必厚亡，故知足不辱，知止不殆，可以长久。"以及第四十六章："天下有道，却走马以粪；天下无道，戎马生于郊。罪莫大于可欲，祸莫大于不知足，咎莫大于欲得。故知足之足，恒足矣。"

蜘蛛别名"喜蛛"，取字"喜"，再加上某物自天而降的表现形态，合之为"喜从天降"。蜘蛛有八条腿，"八"字谐音"发"，寓意财源滚滚、升官发财、八面来财、八面玲珑。世人佩戴和田玉蜘蛛，寓意节节高升，为人处世八面玲珑，在事业上有所成就。"蜘蛛"的谐音为"知足"，可寄托人们寻求生活与精神上的满足，从而令自己的品性与内心达到知足。另外，蜘蛛也是勤劳的代表，它们为了捕捉到食物而不停地织网，表现出它为了目标会不停地奋斗努力，所以也喻示着人们要想得到回报，就要努力耕耘。

知足常乐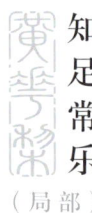
（局部）

Satisfied with What One Has

Length: 10 cm　Width: 7 cm　Height: 3.5 cm　Weight: 117.1 g　Sculptor: Bai Ji

Spider
By Hong Zikui of the Song Dynasty

The sun is already setting,
And it is too late to leave.
A great, criss-crossing web hangs overhead,
Cobwebs are arranged from top to bottom.
Its belly is like a gourd, fat, with flying insects inside.
Its mouthpart carries a poisonous sting, good for boring.
Morning comes and it is suddenly swept away by a child,
Not even the cracks of the ledges are left alone.

The idea of being satisfied with what one has originates from the Taoist School and, afterwards, as is widely known, it became a gem of Chinese traditional culture. Collectable items often have this kind of subject matter carved into them. The most-commonly-seen way of expressing this is by carving a spider on a foot. This is a piece carved from native Chinese scented rosewood by Bai Ji. It carries a simple atmosphere. The arrangement is elaborate, causing people to love it so much they would not want to part from it. Being satisfied with what one has, at the earliest, comes from the forty-fourth chapter of *Tao Te Ching*: "Which is more amiable, life or reputation? Which is more precious, reputation or material wealth? Which is more harmful, loss or gain? Excessive love of fame and profit will demand a higher price; excessive accumulation of wealth is bound to lead to an even more disastrous loss. As such, if you understand satisfaction, you won't be humiliated. If you understand when to stop, you won't encounter danger. In this way, you can persevere for a long time, safe and sound." And the forty-sixth chapter stated:"If everything under the heaven were governed in accordance with 'dao', a warhorse would be used to till the land; if everything under heaven were not governed in accordance with 'dao', even a pregnant horse would be sent to the outskirts of a battlefield to birth a colt. The greatest mistake is greed. The greatest disaster is not knowing satisfaction. As such, those who know when to be satisfied will always be satisfied."

Spiders are also called "xi zhu". If you take the same character "xi" (meaning "joy" or "to be fond of") and add the phrase "fall from heaven", you get the phrase "joy from the heaven". Spiders have eight legs. "Eight" ("ba") and "to make money" ("fa") are similar in sounds. It symbolizes profits pour in from all sides, to be promoted and gain wealth, wealth coming from eight directions, or everything going smoothly. People wear nephrite spiders. It signifies receiving promotions step by step, everything going smoothly, or success in one's career. Spider ("zhi zhu") and "to know satisfaction" ("zhi zu") are homonyms. It helps people seek satisfaction in their life and spirit, allowing their nature and heart to reach satisfaction. In addition, spiders also represent diligence. In order to catch prey, they weave a web incessantly. It shows their great and unceasing effort to achieve their objective. Therefore, it can be used as a metaphor for people working hard to receive a return.

参禅入定

参禅入定

长：8.5厘米　宽：7厘米　高：19.5厘米　重：265.5克　款：九品

题雪花达摩布衣偈（节选）
宋·家铉翁

拈花公案且莫道，西来正被拈花恼。
一花开后几花开，微笑不禁成绝倒。
归去来，人未老，掉下从前旧草鞋。
衲被蒙头面壁坐，提起不直一落索。

这件雕件所用材质是一块越黄老料，其棕眼较多，油性一般，后经九品改刀后化瑕疵为珍品，神采毕现。其上雕绘的是达摩参禅图，辅刻以上方一轮圆月，是为达摩成佛时的光环。

曾经，达摩问道于其师般若多罗，说："我得到佛法以后，应到何地传化？"般若多罗答曰："你应该去震旦（中国）。"又说："你到震旦以后，不要住在南方，那里的君主喜好功业，不能领悟佛理。"达摩后用三年时间，渡海翻山，历尽艰难曲折抵达东土。北魏孝昌三年（527），达摩上少林寺，之后便在少林寺旁不远的嵩山西麓五乳峰的中峰上部，离绝顶不远的一孔天然石洞中面壁九年，修行坐禅，终开辟出为东土人民所接受和传播的法门：东土禅宗。

达摩的典故众多，流传较广的有"一苇渡江""面壁九年""断臂立雪""只履西归"等，这些美丽的传奇，表达了后人对达摩祖师的敬仰和怀念。

一苇渡江

传说达摩渡长江时，风急雨骤，烟波浩渺，无一船可搭，其便在江岸折芦苇一根，法相峻然立于其上，渡过了长江。现今少林寺尚存有达摩"一苇渡江"的石刻画碑。而另一种流传的说法是达摩和梁武帝谈论佛事之后，得知达摩已离去，梁武帝懊悔不已，立即派人骑骠追赶。追至幕府山中段时，两边山峰突然闭合，一行人被夹在两峰之间，达摩此时正至江边，见有人赶来，就在江边折芦苇一根投入江中，化一叶扁舟，飘然过江。

面壁九年

北魏孝昌三年，达摩抵达少林寺，藏身于嵩山西麓五乳峰的中峰离绝顶不远的一孔天然石洞中，其时法身正坐，两腿曲盘，两手作弥陀印，双目下视，五心朝天入定，每次开定，仅起身做一些径行活动，锻炼一下身体，待倦怠恢复后，又坐禅入定，如是进行了长达九年的面壁坐禅。最终其开辟东土禅宗一脉，为东土人士所接纳传播。禅宗的核心是摒除语言，直达心性，寻找契机悟道成佛，传说禅宗六祖慧能大师，本不识字，某天于菩提树下参禅，心见菩提，便证道成佛，他留下的一首佛偈在禅宗近两千年的历史上，启发了无数后来人，是为：

　　菩提本无树，明镜亦非台。
　　本来无一物，何处惹尘埃。

断臂立雪

相传嵩山有位名叫神光的僧人，听说达摩大师住在少林寺，于是前往拜谒问佛之事。达摩面壁端坐，不置可否。神光没有气馁，暗自思忖："古人求道，无不历尽艰难险阻，忍常人所不能忍。古人尚且如此，我有何德何能？当自勉励！"时值寒冬腊月，纷纷扬扬漫天大雪。夜幕降临，神光仍在寺外站立不动，天明积雪已没过他的双膝。达摩这时才开口问道："你久立雪中，所求何事？"神光泪流满面说道："只愿和尚慈悲，为我传道。"达摩担心神光只是一时冲动，难以持久，略有迟疑。神光明白达摩心思，便取利刃自断左臂，置于达摩面前。达摩至此便将其留在身边，取法名慧可。

少林寺内的立雪亭，便是为纪念慧可断臂求法的事迹而建。达摩禅师后来以四卷《楞伽经》授予慧可，达摩逝后，慧可便成为禅宗在东土的第二代祖师，自此，禅宗在中国有了传法世系。

只履西归

达摩圆寂，世人震惊。然而东魏使臣宋云因事出使西域，许久未归，对达摩圆寂的事一无所知。达摩圆寂后两年，宋云从西域返回洛京（洛阳），途经葱岭的时候，见达摩一手挂着锡杖，一手掂着一只鞋子，身穿僧衣，赤着双脚，由东往西而来。宋云急忙停步问道："大师，你往哪里去？"达摩答曰："我往西天去。"

宋云回京后，向皇帝复命交旨，顺便提到他途经葱岭遇见达摩老祖回西天的事情。东魏孝静帝怒斥宋云："人所共知，达摩大师死于禹门，葬于熊耳山，造塔定林寺，你怎么说在葱岭遇见了大师？这分明是欺君，岂有此理！"宋云先叩头，后说话："皇上容禀：葱岭见达摩，祖师光着脚，一手挂锡杖，一手提只履，僧衣随风飘，翩翩向西行，称要回西天去，并嘱咐我不要将这件事说出去，假若说出去，便会有灾祸，臣以为是戏言，兼之不敢欺瞒圣上，便如实奏陈。臣所言，句句是真，不敢欺圣上，万望圣察。"孝静帝听了以后，无所适从。群臣道："既然真假是非难辨，可以开棺验证。"孝静帝采纳了建议，遂命人开棺视之，棺中空空，只剩下一只鞋子，方知大师真的已经化身成佛。现今少林寺碑廊内，还留有一块《达摩只履西归圆碑》，上边刻有四句佛偈：

　　达摩入灭太和年，熊耳山中塔庙全。
　　不是宋云葱岭见，谁知只履去西天。

Entering Meditation

Length: 8.5 cm   Width: 7 cm   Height: 19.5 cm   Weight: 265.5 g   Sculptor: Jiu Pin

The Song of a Cloth-clad Monk (Dharma) in the Snowflake （Excerpts）
By Jia Xuanweng of the Song Dynasty

The kindred koan had not yet spoken,
But his kindred spirit distressed the man from the West who came to rectify.
After one flower blooms, many flowers bloom.
His smile could not be kept from bursting out in laughter.
Going and coming, Dharma Master doesn't seem to be getting old,
An old straw sandal fell down.
Covering head with a quilt and sitting face the wall, Holding shoes in hand.

This carving is made of aged Vietnamese scented rosewood. The wood grain has many flecks. The oiliness is average. The sculptor, Jiu Pin, altered the piece, and transformed its blemishes into a valuable object, showing its spirit completely. The carving depicts an image of Dharma in meditation. There is a full moon at the top, complimenting the image. It is a halo of the Dharma attaining enlightenment.

Once, Bodhidharma asked his master, Boreduoluo, "After I obtain Dharma, where should I go to pass it on?" Boreduoluo replied, "You should go to Zhendan (that is, China)." He again said, "After you arrive in Zhendan, you should not live in the south. The monarchs there are fond of achievements. They can not understand Buddhism." It took Bodhidharma three years, to cross over seas and mountains and experience difficulties and complications to arrive in the East. He was in the 3rd year of Xiaochang of Wei of the Northern Dynasties (386–534). Bodhidharma went to the Shaolin Temple. Afterwards, in a natural cave not far from the highest peak of Mt. Song nearby the Shaolin Temple, he sat in meditation and faced the cavern walls for nine years. At last, he set out for the people that would accept and disseminate the gates of enlightenment: Eastern Zen Buddhism.

The stories about Bodhidharma are numerous and have spread far and wide, "A Reed Crossing the River," "Nine Years of Meditation", "Cutting Off One's Arm in the Snow", "Going West with One Shoe", etc. These beautiful legends express the reverence and reminiscence later generations had towards Bodhidharma.

A Reed Crossing the River

Legend says that when Bodhidharma was crossing the Yangtze River, there was a strong wind and sudden rain and a vast mist covered the water. He had no boat to take. He broke a reed on the shore. His appearance was phenomenal. He stood upon it and crossed the river. Today, the Shaolin Temple still has retained in storage a stone inscription monument of Bodhidharma's "A Reed Crossing the River." Another legend says that after Bodhidharma and Emperor Liang Wu discussed Buddhism, when he found out that Bodhidharma had already left, Emperor Liang Wu felt endless remorse. He immediately dispatched people to ride mules and pursue him. When they pursued him to the middle of the Mu Fu mountains, the two mountain peaks suddenly closed together. One of the parties was crushed in between. Bodhidharma at this point made straight for the river bank. He saw someone rushing over, so he broke a reed and threw it into the river, forming a small boat, and he floated across.

Nine Years of Meditation

He was in the 3rd year of Xiaochang of Wei of the Northern Dynasties. After Bodhidharma arrived at the Shaolin Temple, he hid in a natural cave not far from the highest peak of Mt. Song nearby. Then, he sat in a straight, meditative stance, his legs crossed atop each other, his hands making the sign of the Amitabha, and both eyes looking down. He entered into a "five hearts to heaven" stance (palms of the hands, bottom of the feet,

参禅入定
（局部）

152

and top of the head are facing upward). Each time he ended the meditation, he would only get up to do physical exercises. After being exhausted, he would again resume a state of meditation. He did this for nine years facing the walls of the cave. At last he set up a vein of Eastern Zen Buddhism for those in the East that would admit and disseminate Buddhism. The core of Zen Buddhism dismisses language, seeking nonstop an opportunity to comprehend the path to enlightenment through nature. Legend says that Huineng, the Sixth Patriarch of Zen Buddhism, was illiterate. One day while he was practicing meditation underneath a bodhi tree, he saw bodhi, confirming his path to enlightenment. He left behind a Buddhist hymn with close to 2,000 years of history, enlightening countless people afterwards. The hymn goes: The Bodhi roots have no tree, and the mirror has no stand; Originally there was not one thing, where was the dust stirred.

Cutting Off One's Arm in the Snow
According to the legend, there was a monk called the Shen Guang on Mt. Song. He heard that Bodhidharma's master lived at the Shaolin Temple, so Hence, he went to pay him a visit to inquire about Buddhist matters. Bodhidharma sat upright facing the wall and refused to speak. The Shen Guang was not discouraged, but pondered within himself, "People from the ancient times pursued the path, all of whom experienced untold dangers and difficulties. They endured what ordinary people could not have endured. That's what people used to do. I am not good enough, I should spur myself!" It was during the cold and winter months and there was a lot of snow all over the sky. At nightfall, the Shen Guang was still standing motionless outside the temple. At dawn, the snow had covered up to his knees. Bodhidharma, at this time, spoke, "You have been standing in the snow for a long time. What are you seeking?" The Shen Guang, with tears streaming down his cheeks, replied, "Only the mercy of the Buddhist monk that you would expound the wisdom of ancient sages." Bodhidharma worried that the Shen Guang was merely acting on impulse for a time. It would be difficult to last, and so he hesitated. The Shen Guang understood Bodhidharma's thoughts, so he then took a sharp blade and cut off his own left arm in front of Bodhidharma. Bodhidharma now stayed by his side and gave him the name "Hui Ke"("Intelligent").
Inside the Shaolin Temple, a pavilion was built to commemorate Hui Ke's deed, cutting off his own arm, to seek Buddhist teaching. Bodhidharma's honorific title was later given to Hui Ke in the fourth volume, *Lengqie Sutra*. After Bodhidharma passed away, Hui Ke become the second forefather of Eastern Zen Buddhism. Since then, Zen Buddhism had a lineage being passed down in China.

Going West with One Shoe.
People were shocked at Bodhidharma's death. Yet, Easter Wei of the Northern Dynastyes (534–550) sent Song Yun Dynasties to the Western Regions on a diplomatic mission. He did not come back for a long time and knew nothing about Bodhidharma's death. Two years after Bodhidharma passed away, Song Yun returned from the Western Regions. When he was passing through the Pamir Plateau, he saw Bodhidharma leaning on a monk's staff with one hand and the other hand holding shoes. He wore monk's clothing and was barefoot. He was coming from the east heading towards the west. Song Yun stopped hastily and asked, "Master, where are you going?" Bodhidharma replied, "I'm going to the Western Paradise."
After Song Yun returned to the capital, he reported back to the emperor. He mentioned that he had seen Bodhidharma heading to the Western Paradise when he passed through the Pamir Plateau. Emperor Xiao Jing of Easter Wei of the Northern Dynasties angrily rebuked Song Yun, "Everyone knows Bodhidharma died at Yu Gate. He was buried at Mt. Xiong'er and a pavilion was set up in the Shaolin Temple. How can you say you met him in the Pamir Plateau? You are clearly trying to deceive the monarch. How can this be so?" Song Yun first bowed and then said, "Emperor, allow me to report: I met Bodhidharma in the Pamir Plateau. He was barefoot. He leaned on a monk's staff with one hand and the other carried only one shoe. His clothes floated in the wind and he walked gracefully westward. He said that he was heading to the Western Paradise and that I should not tell others of this matter. If I were to speak of it, a disaster could arise. I thought he was joking and dared not fool the emperor. I made a statement according to the facts. Every word I have said is true. I dare not deceive the emperor. Look and observe." After Emperor Xiao Jing listened, he was at a loss of what to do. The count said, "Since it is difficult to debate whether it is true or false, you can open up his (Bodhidharma's) coffin and inspect inside." Emperor Xiao Jing accepted his proposal. They proceeded to order someone to open the coffin and look inside. The coffin was empty with only one shoe inside. They realized that the great master really had reincarnated. Today inside the monument at the Shaolin Temple, there remains a block, "The Round Monument of Bodhidharma Returning West with one Shoe" with the following inscribed Buddhist hymn:
"Bodhi Dharma died during the Taihe period, when Baota Temple was untouched/complete in Xiong'er Mountain. If it weren't for Song Yun at the Pamir Plateau, who would have known he returned to the Western Paradise with only one shoe."

三多佛手

三多佛手

长:30厘米 宽:8厘米 高:6厘米 重:334克 款:九品

佛手花

宋·杨巽斋

丹葩点漆细馨浮,苍叶轻排指样柔。
香案净瓶安顿了,还能摩顶济人不。

这件《三多佛手》来历曲折,品相精美,是我极钟爱的一件雕件。十几年前,我刚开始入迷黄花梨。每天大部分时间都沉浸在木头的世界中,周默的《木鉴:中国古典家具用材鉴赏》反反复复翻看了很多遍,也通过网络结交了很多黄花梨的商家和玩家,这件佛手的原料便是来自一位海南当地玩家。料到手后发现其已经开好了窗,料质细腻,棕眼全无,降香浓郁,属于八所地区的沉水土埋老料。但那时圈子太小,认识的工匠有限,便糊涂地交由一位河北的匠人打造。耗时三月有余,但成品的佛手却工艺粗糙,毫无设计,完全是暴殄天物。可木已成舟,便将之封藏于盒中,多年未曾见光。后来有幸结识北京"而立文玩"的任兄,从他熟识的能工巧匠中挑了一位,帮忙妙手回春,重新改刀。三个月之后,任兄发来消息,称赞改刀后的作品可谓"叹为观止,惊为天人"。

整件作品取名为《三多佛手》,其由仙桃、石榴和佛手三部分构成,仙桃寓意多寿,石榴寓意多子,佛手寓意多福,因此称为"三多"。整件作品在细节上精雕细琢,每一节枝干都苍遒有力,每一片叶子都纤毫毕现,佛手的处理更是温润婉致、大气饱满。

"三多"中的石榴自古以来便被中国人所熟知,"八月十五月正南,瓜果石榴列满盘"便是中国一句流传甚广的传统民谚。同时,在佛教文化中亦有共识:"石榴一花多果,一房千实,故为吉祥果,一切供果之中,石榴为最上品。"

而佛手柑一名"飞穰",树似柑而叶尖长,结实形如佛手,其皮生绿、熟黄,虽味短而香馥最久,置之室内笥中其香不散,因此其干品除了作药材,也常常在文玩圈内作清供用。"佛手"谐音"福寿",幸福长寿,形状上也的确像极了佛祖的手型,常被视作大吉之物。

仙桃则在中国传统文化中流传更广,是长寿多福、禄位高升的意思。仙桃生在仙界,据说是王母娘娘招待众神仙的上等贡品,需三千年一开花,三千年一结果,非常珍贵,因此民间很早就用桃来作为多福多寿的象征。

三多佛手
（局部）

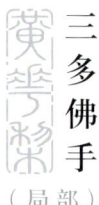

Three "Mores" of Buddha's Hands

Length: 30 cm   Width: 8 cm   Height: 6 cm   Weight: 334 g   Sculptor: Jiu Pin

The Flower of Buddha's Hands
By Yang Xunzhai of Song Dynasty

The beautiful citrus medica sarcodactylis flower carries a pleasant fragrance.
And its Buddha's hand-shaped fruit is lovely surrounded by green leaves.
As the fruit is an offering on the incense table, will it be able to bring blessings to humans?

The piece "Three 'Mores' of Buddha's Hands" has a complicated history. The appearance is refined. It is one carving that I am extremely fond of. More than ten years ago, I had just begun to be fascinated by scented rosewood. Almost every day, I was immersed in the world of wood. I repeatedly browsed many times through Zhou Mo's *A Guide on Wood*. I also made many friends with businessmen and collectors through the Internet. The material of "Three 'Mores' of Buddha's Hands" comes from a local collector in Hainan Province. After I had obtained the material, I realized it had already been sampled. The material is exquisite with no flecks and a rich aroma. It belongs to the aged material buried in soil and can sink in water in Basuo Town. However, at that time my circle was small and my knowledge of artisans was limited. In confusion, I handed it over to a craftsman in Hebei Province for him to work on. It took more than three months, but the finished result of the Buddha's Hands was crude and completely lacking design. It was a total reckless waste of natural resources. Nevertheless, what is done can not be undone. As such, it was stored away in a box and hasn't been taken out for many years. Afterwards, fortunately, I met Ren at Beijing Er Li. Being well acquainted with his skilled workmanship, I dug the piece up and he found a skilled sculptor to bring it back to "life", transforming the object once more. After three months, Ren sent news. The transformed work could be praised as causing one to "gasp in amazement and be astounded at such beauty".

The entire product is called "Three 'Mores' of Buddha's Hands". It consists of the peaches of immortality, pomegranates, and Buddha's Hands (also called fingered citron; literally "Buddha's Hands" in Chinese). The peaches of immortality signify more life, the pomegranates signify more children ("child" and "seed" are similar in Chinese; pomegranates have many seeds), and the Buddha's Hands signify more happiness ("Buddha" and "happiness" sound similar in Chinese). Therefore, it is called "Three 'Mores'". The detail in this entire piece was finely carved and cut with precision. Every branch has boundless power, every minute detail of every leaf is complete and apparent, and the Buddha's Hands, full of style, are handled with even more grace and gentleness.

Since the ancient times, people have been well acquainted with the pomegranates in "Three 'Mores'". "At the Mid-Autumn Festival night when the moon is full, bounty of melons and fruits are served on the table." It is precisely the folk saying that spread widely throughout China. At the same time, Buddhist culture also has a common understanding as can be seen here: "Pomegranates bear lots of fruit. A pomegranate has a thousand seeds. As such, it is a lucky fruit. Out of all fruits, pomegranates are above all."

Buddha's Hands are also called "fei rang". The stem resembles a tangerine and the leaves are pointed and long. It has a strong appearance, just like Buddha's hands. The skin is green when raw and turns yellow when it is ripe. The taste is short, but the sweet fragrance lasts long. If it is stored indoors in a container, its aroma is not lost. Thus, aside from using it dried out as medicine, in cultural collector item circles, it is also frequently used for aromatherapy. Buddha's Hands and "happiness and longevity" are homonyms. Its shape extremely resembles Buddha's hands. It is often regarded as a very auspicious item.

The peaches of immortality, in Chinese traditional culture, are even more widespread. They symbolize longevity, more happiness, and the promotion of rank and salary. The peaches of immortality, in mythology, are said to have been the highest quality tribute to the Queen Mother of the West from the deities. It blooms once in three millennium and then bears one fruit. As such, it is especially precious. People at a very early time used peaches as a symbol for happiness and long life.

鱼跃龙门

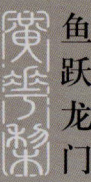

鱼跃龙门

长：9.5厘米　宽：7.5厘米　高：12.5厘米　重：63.9克　款：九品

赠崔侍郎

唐·李白

黄河三尺鲤，本在孟津居。
点额不成龙，归来伴凡鱼。
故人东海客，一见借吹嘘。
风涛倘相见，更欲凌昆墟。

　　本件作品为海南黄花梨一块边角小料所雕。海南黄花梨目前由于原料枯竭，市场上越来越难得，即便偶有出售，价格也是居高不下。在此情况下，本品采用的是一小块黄花梨的边角小料，经过匠人的精细加工，成为一件不错的艺术品，可谓化腐朽为神奇。这同时也贴合了中国古代手工艺中有效利用原料的优良传统：将制大物件刨下来的边角料收集起来，稍大的可以做摆件，小的做手把件，长的做镇纸，短的做文牌，即使是粉末都可以加工成香。

　　"鱼跃龙门"的故事古文中多有记载，宋代《埤雅·释鱼》说："俗说鱼跃龙门，过而为龙，唯鲤或然。"《太平广记·卷四六六》"龙门"条引《三秦记》则载有："龙门山，在河东界。禹凿山断门阔一里余。黄河自中流下，两岸不通车马……每岁季春，有黄鲤鱼，自海及诸川，争来赴之。一岁中，登龙门者，不过七十二。初登龙门，即有云雨随之，天火自后烧其尾，乃化为龙矣。"而清代张澍辑《三秦记》复云："江海大鱼薄集龙门下，数千，不得上。上则为龙，不上者鱼，故云曝腮龙门。"

　　后世民间传说，遂谓为"鲤鱼跃龙门"。人们常用"登龙门"来比喻因得到有力者的援引而致显耀。科举时代，参加会试获得进士功名的也被称作为"登龙门"。"鲤鱼跃龙门"，既是优美传说的形象表述，更寄托着祈盼飞跃高升、一朝交运的美好愿望，尤其是那些指望子弟靠读书应试博取功名前程的人家，都把它当作幸运来临的象征。

鱼跃龙门（局部）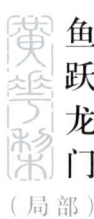

Fish Jumping through Dragon Gate

Length: 9.5 cm   Width: 7.5 cm   Height: 12.5 cm   Weigth: 63.9 g   Sculptor: Jiu Pin

Dedicated to Cui Shi Lang
By Li Bai of the Tang Dynasty

In Yellow River swam a three-foot carp,
Who originally lived in Meng River.
He failed to jump over the Dragon Gate,
Coming back to a couple common fish.
They were his old acquaintances,
And he thanked them for their praise and admiration.
For a good chance to flourish,
He wished he could soar to the highest top of Mount Kunlun.

This piece is carved from a corner of a block of Chinese scented rosewood. Due to the material being used up, Chinese scented rosewood is becoming more and more seldom seen in the marketplace, and the selling prices remain high. Under these circumstances, this product utilized scraps from scented rosewood. After fine processing by the craftsman, it has become a pretty good art piece. It could even be said that he turned something rotten into something magical. At the same time, he adjusted the piece closely according to ancient handicrafts of China, effectively using the first-rate, traditional material. He gathered the scraps scraped off of a bigger object. A somewhat bigger piece can be used for display and a smaller one can be held in the hand. A long one can be used as paperweight and a short one can be used as a charm. Even a fine powder can be processed into something fragrant.

Many stories of "Fish Leaping through the Dragon Gate" are mentioned in classical prose. *Pi Ya Explaining Fish* from the Song Dynasty states, "Custom says fish leap through the Dragon Gate, passing through and becoming a dragon. Only carp could do this." The "Dragon Gate" in *Volume 466 of Extensive Records of the Taiping Era* is originally from *Record of Three Qins*. It records, "Dragon Gate Mountain is located in the East River. Yu (a mythical figure who was the king of the ancient China) cut the mountain in half and forged a passage way shaped like a gate which stretched over a mile. The Yellow River flowed through the break in the mountain, and the river banks on the two sides could not be passed by horses and vehicles...Every year in late spring there were yellow carps rushing from the sea to the rivers. In a year, there were no more than 72 carps jumping over the cliff. As soon as a carp passed over the Dragon Gate, a cluster of clouds and rain followed it. The heavenly fire burned its tail from behind and it turned into a dragon..." Zhang Shu from the Qing Dynasty edited *Record of Three Qins* stated, "Big fish of seas and rivers gather below the Dragon Gate. Thousands could not come up. Ones that could come up became dragons. Ones that could not, remained fish. That's why it is called the setback by the Dragon Gate."

Popular tradition of later generations thereupon used the phrase "a carp leaping through the Dragon Gate". People often use this phrase "ascending the Dragon Gate" as a metaphor to show off power one obtained. During the time of imperial examinations, successful candidates who obtained the scholarly honor were called "ascending the Dragon Gate". Carp leaping through the Dragon Gate—the beautiful imagery of this legend gives a beautiful desire for quick promotion and luck, and especially a hope for children to win scholarly honor in school and have a future career. It is a symbol of approaching fortune.

竹节蝙蝠
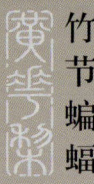

竹节蝙蝠

高：18厘米　直径：7厘米　重：211.5克

蝙蝠洞

宋·倪梦龙

悬崖多蝙蝠，往往寿千年。
自古人难到，如今尔得先。
所餐崖上乳，不出瓮中天。
自有攀援者，曾看抱朴篇。

蝙蝠简称"蝠"，因"蝠"与"福"谐音，人们以"蝠"表示福气、福禄寿喜等祥瑞。民间绘画常以五只蝙蝠寓意五福临门，旧时丝绸锦缎常以蝙蝠图形为花纹。婚嫁、寿诞等喜庆时日，妇女们头上戴的绒花和一些服饰、器物上也常用蝙蝠造型。

古人认为蝙蝠是天上的老鼠，《艺文类聚》上载有："方言曰蝙蝠自关而东，谓之服翼，或谓之飞鼠，或谓老鼠，或谓之仙鼠。自关而西秦陇之间谓蝙蝠。"而《书·洪范》关于五福则这样说："五福：一曰寿，二曰富，三曰康宁，四曰攸好德，五曰考终命。"《抱朴子》一书中也有关于蝙蝠的描述："千岁蝙蝠，色如白雪，集则倒悬，脑重故也。此物得而阴干末服之，令人寿万岁。"唐朝大诗人元稹《景申秋八首（其二）》一诗中亦有关于蝙蝠的名句："帘断萤火入，窗明蝙蝠飞"。

竹节蝙蝠
（局部）

Bat on Bamboo

Height: 18 cm Diameter: 7 cm Weigth: 211.5 g

Bat Cave
By Ni Menglong of the Song Dynasty

There are many bats in the cliff,
And they tend to live for thousands of years.
Humankind has never lived so long,
But now these bats have made it.
They ate the dew on the cliff,
And they never walk out of that place.
There are people who climbed the mountains,
And they must have read Baopuzi, believing the ba could bring longevity to them.

Bat ("bian fu"), can be abbreviated as "fu". Because bat ("fu") and happiness (also "fu") are homonyms, people use bats to express good fortune, an auspicious sign of happiness, long life, etc. People often paint five bats together, signifying five blessings (longevity, wealth, health, virtue, and a natural death). In former times, silk cloth brocades often had decorative designs of bats. During marriage, birth, and such festival, women wore velvet flowers and adornment, on whic. bat designs were commonly used.

People of ancient times believed bats to be celestial rats. *Yiwen Leiju* wrote, "Dialect calls it bat. In northeast China, it is called Fu Yi, or flying squirrel, or rat, or celestial rat. In northwest China, between the Qinling Mountains and Long Mountains, it is called bat." *Shu-Hong Fan*, in regard to the five joys, writes, "Five joys: the first is longevity, the second is wealth, the third is health, the fourth is virtue, and the fifth is a natural death." *Baopuzi* also has a description of bats, "The bat has lived for a thousand years; their color is white as snow. They gather together and, because of their heavy head, they hang upside down. If you catch such a bat, dry it in the shade, then grind it to fine powder and take it as a tonic, allowing for long life." Yuan Zhen, a Chinese poet in the middle Tang Dynasty, wrote a famous saying about bats in his poem in Qing Shen Qiu (Volume 2) "Fireflies come into the room through broken curtains, and bats fly around near the bright window."

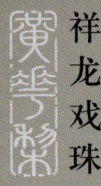

祥龙戏珠

祥龙戏珠

长：10厘米　宽：9厘米　高：8厘米　重：229克　款：九品

七律

清·金准

碧天楼阁带春星，槛外飞泉坐倒听。
树色湿云诸洞黑，磬声摇月数峰青。
院中宿鸟参禅定，池上游龙学佛灵。
顿觉前身金粟是，悬灯萝幌独翻经。

这件《祥龙戏珠》作品是由一块糠梨做雕，其描绘的是一条祥龙腾空而起，中间托起一颗明珠，下则辅雕以惊涛拍岸，寓意为祥龙在东海之上嬉戏一颗刚刚升起的明珠。

我们通常所见的龙戏珠的珠子多是带着火焰，像是一个火球，其表现的是从东海中升起的太阳。那既然是太阳出海，为什么要龙来"戏"呢？这里要引入古人眼中的"四方神"：东方青龙，西方白虎，南方朱雀，北方玄武。太阳是从东方升起的，而龙则是代表东方的神物，这样，祥龙戏珠就有太阳崇拜的意思了，是太阳崇拜和龙崇拜的交融。

通常我们所见的多是二龙戏珠，因在古人的理解中龙分雌雄，如果珠作卵解，那么就是父母双方共同呵护、爱抚他们的子女；如果珠作太阳解，则是雌雄二龙共迎旭日东升，让灿烂的阳光普照大地。再者，二龙对称，龙体弯长，珠形滚圆，在构图上也更富审美上的愉悦感。

祥龙戏珠（局部）

An Auspicious Dragon Playing with a Pearl

Length: 10 cm Width: 9 cm Height: 8 cm Weight: 229 g Sculptor: Jiu Pin

Seven-Syllable Poem
By Jin Zhun of the Qing Dynasty

Sitting in the pavilion, you can see the spring stars in the clear sky,
And hear the sound of the spring flowing down the window.
Trees, clouds and caves are stained black by the night,
And the sound of chime stone spreads with the moonlight through green mountain peaks.
The birds in the yard do not move as if they are practicing meditation,
And the kois swimming in the lake seem to be learning Dharma.
Suddenly I feel that I am the reincarnation of Jinsu Rulai Buddha,
While reading the scriptures alone under the lamp in the tent.

This piece, "An Auspicious Dragon Playing with a Pearl", was carved from dry scented rosewood. It depicts an auspicious dragon soaring upwards. Rising out of the middle is a pearl and below, complimenting the carving, are stormy waves beating against the shore. It depicts a dragon playing with a pearl that has just risen out of the East China Sea.

The pearls we often see being played with by dragons are usually ignited, like a ball of fire. It shows the sun rising out of the East China Sea. If the sun is coming out of the sea, why does the dragon come out and "play" then? This pulls us into the four gods in the eyes of people from ancient times: the emerald dragon of the east, the white tiger of the west, the vermillion bird of the south, and the black tortoise of the north. The sun rises from the east. Dragons represent a mythological creature of the East. In this way, an auspicious dragon playing with a pearl has a meaning of adoration towards the sun. It is a blend of adoration towards the sun and adoration towards dragons.

Normally, we see two dragons playing with a pearl, because in the understanding of people of ancient times, dragons were divided into male and female. If the pearl was seen as an egg, then it was a common blessing of the father and the mother affectionately caring for their children. If the pearl were seen as the sun, the male and the female dragons are both welcoming the sun rising from the east, letting the earth bathe in the brilliant sunshine. Moreover, two dragons are symmetrical, their bodies are long and twisting, and the pearl's shape is round. From a compositional viewpoint, it is more aesthetically pleasing.

醉卧达摩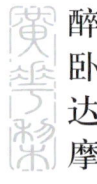

醉卧达摩

长：17厘米　宽：15.5厘米　高：3.5厘米　重：121.7克　款：九品

戏题时贤画达摩像六段

当代·启功

片苇东航，只履西归，教外之传。

要本心直指，不凭文字，一衣一钵，面壁多年。

敬问嘉宾，有何贵干，枯坐居然叫作禅。

谁知道，竟一花五叶，法统蝉联。

断肢二祖心虔。又行者逃生命缕悬。

忆菩提非树，那椿公案，触而且背，早落言诠。

临济开宗，逢人便打，寂静如何变野蛮。

空留下，漫装腔作势，各相俱全。

　　这件作品《醉卧达摩》，由海黄糠梨老料雕刻而成，描绘的是达摩祖师枕靠在一个布袋上，布袋上摊有经书一本。这件糠梨的油性非常好，更没有一般老料的棕眼，是糠梨中的极品，辅以九品神俊的雕工，可谓相得益彰。

　　达摩为中国禅宗初祖，其南朝宋末从印度乘船来到中国，于广州登陆，然后北行至北魏，到处以禅法教人。据说他曾在洛阳看见永宁寺宝塔建筑的精美，自言年已一百五十岁，历游各国都不曾见过，于是"口唱南无，合掌连日"（《洛阳伽蓝记》卷一）。

　　达摩在少林寺传法慧可之后，即到熊耳山下的定林寺传法五年，于梁武帝大同二年（536）圆寂，终年一百五十岁。众僧徒悲痛之极，依佛礼将初祖大师葬于定林寺内，并修建了达摩灵塔和达摩殿。梁武帝萧衍亲自撰写了题为《菩提达摩大师颂并序》的碑文，以示对达摩大师创立禅宗的纪念。后来东魏使臣于元象元年（538）自西域取经返回途中，遇见达摩大师杖挑只履西归，立即报于皇帝。皇帝闻之，命人挖开达摩墓葬，只见只履空棺，方知大师已脱化成佛，遂将定林寺更名为"空相寺"。

醉卧达摩（局部）

Bodhidharma, Drunk and Lying Down

Length: 17 cm   Width: 15.5 cm   Height: 3.5 cm   Weight: 121.7 g   Sculptor: Jiu Pin

Six Poems for the Dharma Pictures Painted by Shi Xian
By Qi Gong of the Contemporary Era

Dharma traveled eastward in a small reed and go west with one shoe,
Which was what he passed on in addition to his doctrine.
He studied Buddhism by virtue of his sincere heart,
Not by virtue of scriptures and classics, just such a monk's dress,
A Buddhist bowl. He mused facing the wall for many years, and devoted himself to the Buddhist study.
When a guest came to Dharma, he asked the guests what he wanted.
And Dharma was asked why sitting doing nothing could also be called meditation.
Who knows? With the interpretation of Buddhist classics and understanding of Buddhist schools,
Dharma ascended to the highest Buddhist status, living very much in seclusion and focusing on Buddhism.
Dharma thought that this was the case with the walker's life.
He recalled the story that Bodhi was not a tree and a Toon case.
He not only knew these allusions very well, but also was able to remember by heart.
After the establishment of Linji school, when they met people, they hit people with irritability.
How did this silent heart gradually lose its tranquility and move towards barbarism?
Only ugliness was left behind, and all the brutalities of the world were revealed.

This item is called "Bodhidharma, Drunk and Lying Down". It is carved from dry, aged Chinese scented rosewood. It depicts the forefather, Bodhidharma, resting his head on a sack. A classic book on Confucianism is spread out on the sack. The oiliness of the dry scented rosewood is very good and it doesn't have ordinary flecks in the wood grain. It is the best quality dry scented rosewood, which compliments Jiu Pin's amazing and talented carving. You could even say they bring out the best in each other.

Bodhidharma is the father of Zen Buddhism in China. He came from India to Guangzhou, China at the end of the Southern Song Dynasties. Then, he went north to Wei of the Northern Dynasties, teaching people about Zen Buddhism. It is said that he once saw the fine construction of the temple pagoda in Yongning from Luoyang, Henan Province. He was almost 150 years old, but he hadn't seen such a beautiful temple, so he exclaimed, "Namas!" and clasped hands day after day.(A *Record of Buddhist Temples in Luoyang*, Volume 1).

After Bodhidharma passing on the doctrines to Hui Ke at the Shaolin Temple, he passed on doctrines at the Dinglin Temple at Mt. Xiong'er for five years. In the second year of Emperor(536) Wu of Liang, he passed away at the age of 150. Many Buddhist monks were extremely grieved. There was a Buddhist ceremony for the forefather and he was buried inside the Dinglin Temple. The Bodhidharma Pagoda and Bodhidharma Palace Hall were built. Emperor Wu of Liang personally wrote the inscription "The Eulogy of Bodhidharma of the Southern Dynasty" to commemorate Bodhidharma's establishment of Zen Buddhism. Afterwards, during the first year of Yuan Xiang in Eastern Wei of the Northern Dynasties(538), the envoy was returning from the Western Regions when he met Bodhidharma holding only a staff and one shoe going west. He immediately reported what he saw to the emperor. The emperor ordered someone to dig up Bodhidharma's grave. Upon finding only one shoe inside his coffin, the emperor realized the great master had attained enlightenment. Thereupon, the Dinglin Temple changed its name to "Kong Xiang Temple"(literally "temple of illusions").

下篇

素器

石瓢壶

壶径：9厘米　长：14厘米　重：202克

醉翁亭记（节选）
宋·欧阳修

醉翁之意不在酒，在乎山水之间也。
山水之乐，得之心而寓之酒也。

黄花梨工艺品中有一种特别的门类，就是"壶"。按说黄花梨做壶，既不可装水，又无法泡茶，实用性较差，但事实上却惹得众多匠人潜心研究，热衷于使用黄花梨制壶。想来大致有以下几点缘由：首先，茶壶器型极为优美。早期制壶多用紫砂，一把漂亮的茶壶不仅赏心悦目，泡茶之余还能把玩在手，器物的质感与手掌的触感相交融，收获了内心的喜悦。其次，茶壶四周往往为光面，正为黄花梨绚烂的花纹提供了展台，美器美图，岂不乐哉？从这一角度来看，同样为珍贵材料的紫檀制作的茶壶，就较少采用素面器型，往往以雕刻为主。再次，"壶"与"福"谐音，"福"是中国传统文化里恒久的追求。手中有壶，等于手中有福，满足了人们追寻幸福的心理。因此，有中国传统的文化取向与审美取向做后盾，黄花梨壶类文玩也就必然成为市场的宠儿。

石瓢壶为紫砂茗器中经典款式，"石瓢"最早称为"石铫"，"铫"在《辞海》中释为"吊子，一种有柄、有流的小烹器"。"铫"从金属器皿变为陶器，最早见于北宋大学士苏轼《试院煎茶》诗："且学公家作名钦，砖炉石铫行相随"。而石瓢壶称呼的真正来历，是顾景舟引用古文"弱水三千，仅饮一瓢"，"石铫"

应称"石瓢"，从此相沿均称"石瓢壶"。

　　这件海南黄花梨紫油梨石瓢壶是从一位仙游友人处获得，原来的主人用一块紫油梨老料开料后发现料质细腻，黑线分明，是极品的海黄料，便请了制壶匠人打造了这把石瓢壶，成器后果然壶型优美，纹理清晰，人见人爱。原主人说，这样的料质，只能靠缘分获得，我总结为："俛得俛失，随缘而作。"

Teapot

Pot's diameter: 9 cm　　Length: 14 cm　　Weight: 202 g

Account of the Inebriate's Pavilion (Excerpt)
By Ouyang Xiu of the Song Dynasty

The drunkard's heart is not in wine, but in the mountains and waters.
The joy of the mountains and waters is felt in the heart and sustained in wine.

There's a special kind of scented rosewood handicraft—the pot. Normally, to use scented rosewood to make pots, not only can you not boil water, you cannot even make tea. The practical use is relatively poor. It has in fact, however, attracted a multitude of artisans to devote themselves to study carefully and it has created a fondness for using scented rosewood to manufacture pots. It is presumably due to roughly the following reasons: Firstly, the shape of the teapot is exceedingly exquisite. During earlier periods, most pots were made from purple sand. A beautiful pot not only warms the heart and delights the eyes, but you can also hold it in your hand after making tea. The texture of the object harmonizes with the touch of your palm, giving you the innermost joy. Secondly, all around the teapot's surface is typically smooth. The side of the scented rosewood features a splendid decorative designs for display—beautiful craftsmanship with beautiful art. How could one be unhappy? From this point of view, the same is made from red sandalwood—a precious material. It seldom adopts an unpatterned form, but rather, more often than not, largely features engravings. Additionally, the Chinese word for "pot" and "happiness" are homonyms. "Happiness" is the persistent goal in Chinese tradition. Holding a pot in your hand equates to holding happiness in your hand. It satisfies people's psychological pursuit of happiness. As a result, there is support for Chinese culture oriented and esthetic oriented tradition. Scented rosewood pot-type cultural relics have also inevitably become a favorite in the marketplace.

Stone teapots are the classic style among purple sand tea utensils. "Shi piao" (stone spout) at the earliest was known as "shi tiao" (stone dipper). "Tiao" (dipper), according to the *Encyclopedic Dictionary*, is a "diao zi—a kind of cooking utensil with a shaft and a scoop". "Tiao" (dipper) changed from a metal utensil into pottery. At the earliest, it can be seen in the great Northern Song Dynasty scholar Su Shi's poem *Decoction of Tea* which reads,"I will follow the dignitary to carry with me a whole set of tea utensils for savoring classy tea." However, the authentic origin of the word stone spout teapot is Gu Jingzhou's quote of a line in an ancient prose, "There are many brooks around but I drink only one spout of it.""Shi tiao" (stone dipper) was renamed "shi piao" (stone spout). Since then, they were all called stone spout teapots.

This type of stone spout teapot, made from Chinese scented rosewood, was obtained from a friend in Xianyou County. After the original owner cut open a piece of the wood, he discovered the quality of the material was exquisite. The black lines in the wood were distinct, and it is the best quality of Chinese scented rosewood. So he asked a craftsman to make a stone spout pot from it. After it was complete, the pot's shape was as elegant as expected, and the grain was distinct, which was loved by all. The former owner said that you can only count on fate to obtain this kind of quality material. I would like to summarize, "You gain and lose by chance because everything is predestined."

素笔筒

筒径：10.4 厘米　高：9.6 厘米　重：288 克

饮湖上初晴后雨二首（其二）
宋·苏轼

水光潋滟晴方好，山色空蒙雨亦奇。
欲把西湖比西子，淡妆浓抹总相宜。

这件黄花梨笔筒由黄花梨油梨老料所制，明式素筒，起线收腰，器型端正；料质温润，色泽金黄，降香迷人。尤其可贵的是桶身的满水波纹，高抛至 7 000 目后，波光粼粼，有水光潋滟之美感。

笔筒的历史，最早源于三国，吴国陆玑《毛诗草木鸟兽虫鱼疏》之《螟蛉有子》篇云："取桑虫负之於木空中，或书简笔筒中，七日而化。"对笔筒记载最多的则是明代文献。明代朱彝尊作《笔筒铭》："笔之在案，或侧或颇，犹人之无仪，筒以束之，如客得家，闲彼放心，归于无邪。"说的是毛笔放在桌案上，有的躺着有的斜着，就像一个人没有仪态一样，看起来很不雅观，如果用笔筒把它们都放在一起，就像浪子有了个家一样，毛笔也有了归宿。描写的是日常生活中的风雅感受。

明晚期著名文人文震亨《长物志》笔筒专条云："（笔筒）湘竹、棕榈者佳，毛竹以古铜镶者为雅，紫檀、乌木、花梨亦间可用。"屠隆的《文房器具笺》笔筒条曰："（笔筒）湘竹为之，以紫檀、乌木棱口镶坐为雅，余不入品。"由此，大多认为现代笔筒从明代开始。

至明晚期和清代，成为文人雅士案头必备。不过明代流行素器，多利用本身的色泽、纹理或棕眼加以表现，故显得大方稳重、古朴典雅，而清代则偏重镂空雕刻等繁复的工艺，两式各有千秋，体现不同时期的文风爱好。

Ming Dynasty-Style Rising Veins Brush Container

Container's Diameter: 10.4 cm　Height: 9.6 cm　Weight: 288 g

Drinking at the West Lake: Sunny, then Rainfall (2)
By Su Shi of the Song Dynasty

Light flickers beautifully in the ripples;
The mountain's appearance is wonderful in the mist and drizzle.
You could compare the West Lake to the beauty, Xishi;
Whether her makeup is light or heavy, both are suitable.

This scented rosewood brush container is made from aged scented rosewood. Its style is from the Ming Dynasty. It sits upright with the veins rising and collecting at its center. The quality is soft, the color and luster are golden yellow, and it has a charming rosewood aroma. The especially precious part of the container's body is that it's filled with rippled veins. After using 7,000 grit high-speed polishing, the gleaming reflection of the sunlight is crystalline. Its beauty is like rays of light reflected rolling waves.

The history of this brush container at the earliest has its origins in the Three Kingdoms periods. Lu Ji from the Wu state (southernmost of the Three Kingdoms) in *Bollworms Have Offspring of Commentary on Botanical and Zoological Terms* in the *Book of Songs* writes, "Put the Sang Insect (citrus long-horned beetle, or Anoplophora chinensis) in a wood hole, on bamboo slips, or in a brush pot, and then it will transform after seven days." However, the brush container was found to be recorded most in documents from the Ming Dynasty (1368–1644). Zhu Yizun from the Ming Dynasty in *Brush Container Inscription* wrote, "Some brushes on the table are lateral, some are inclined, as if one has no manners. The container can bunch them together. It is like a visitor finding a home where he can relax and feel at ease, without guilt." That is to say, writing brushes were placed on the table, some were lying flat and some were lying slanted, as if one was without dignity, appearing very unsightly. If you were to place them together in a brush container, like a prodigal son finding a home, the writing brushes also returned home. He described a sense of sophistication in everyday life.

A famous scholar of the late Ming Dynasty, Wen Zhenheng in an entry in *Treatise on Superfluous* Things states about the brush container, "(The brush container) mottled bamboo, a beautiful palm tree, moso bamboo. Inlaying it with old copper is elegant. Purple sandalwood, ebony, and scented rosewood also can be used." Tu Long in an entry in *A Letter on Study Stationary* states about the brush container, "(The brush container) is made of mottled bamboo. Purple sandalwood can be used. Inlaying the edge of the mouth with ebony is elegant. Anything else is unfitting." From this, most believe modern brush containers came about from the Ming Dynasty. In the late Ming Dynasty and the Qing Dynasty (1644–1911), it had become an essential of the elegant scholar's desk. However, more popular plain wooden utensils of the Ming Dynasty used its color and luster, wood grain, or flecks to add to the display, appearing scholarly and secure. The plainness was elegant. During the Qing Dynasty, on the other hand, more emphasis was placed on hollowed engravings and such complicated techniques. Each has its own merits and each reflects a distinct period's style and interest.

黄花梨茶刀

紫油梨款　长：6.5厘米　糠梨款　长：7.2厘米

茶中杂咏·煮茶
唐·皮日休

香泉一合乳，煎作连珠沸。
时看蟹目溅，乍见鱼鳞起。
声疑松带雨，饽恐生烟翠。
尚把沥中山，必无千日醉。

茶刀，为茶具类，茶具按唐文学家皮日休《茶中杂咏》所列，有"茶坞、茶人、茶笋、茶籝、茶舍、茶灶、茶焙、茶鼎、茶瓯、煮茶。"

提及茶的历史，人们首先肯定想到编著了《茶经》的唐代茶圣陆羽，而跟他同时期还有另一位文学家也沉醉茶道，那就是皮日休。皮日休为晚唐著名诗人、文学家，与陆龟蒙齐名，世称"皮陆"。鲁迅曾赞誉他们的小品文为唐末"一塌糊涂的泥塘里的光彩和锋芒"。

皮日休少年成才，但仕途坎坷，早年嗜好喝酒，而且对于诗歌有沉迷的执着感，故自号"醉吟先生"。32岁那年，皮日休被州官推荐到京城长安参加进士考试，但天性不好官场逢迎的他显然难以被接受，尽管具备才能，但却历经数次赶考，才考取了进士。让人未曾想到的是，最后阻碍皮日休的却是他的个人样貌。因他左眼角下塌，远远看去，就像民间所谓的"独眼龙"，形象不佳，加之又不爱讨巧，因此尽管费力考取了进士，所担任的始终只是小官卑宦。皮日休已知难有施展抱负的日子，便毅然投奔了黄巢起义军。僖宗广明元年（880）十二月，义军攻下长安，黄巢称帝，皮日休被任命为翰林学士。按说这是皮日休人生最高境界了，哪里知道后来却因写了一首诗，得罪黄巢，当即被推出斩首了。

上述诗句为皮日休所著《茶中杂咏》十篇中的《煮茶》，描绘了一番煮茶的情景，表达了作者喜爱茶道，并向往田园生活的情怀。其中一句"尚把沥中山，必无千日醉"，更是以茶代酒的至境好句。

下图是两把海黄茶刀，一把紫油梨，一把糠梨，其中紫油梨那把我尤为喜爱。数年前，我从海南朋友处获得一块霸王岭紫油梨老料，在手中放了一段时间，并不知该做点什么，就赠予了北京任兄。过一年有余，忽从任兄那儿看到一把紫油梨茶刀，器型卓越，颇有眼缘，才知是请了东北韩兄费心定制，所用正是旧日我那块料。于是欣然请回，藏至阁中。

Tea Knives

Purple Oil Rosewood Model   Length: 6.5 cm   Dry Rosewood Model   Length: 7.2 cm

Various Songs of Tea - Boiling Tea
By Pi Rixiu of the Tang Dynasty

A little spring water continually boils.
Bubbles like crab eyes splash. Water like fish scales ripple.
From the foam comes a jade mist, a sound like rain on pine.
Drinking that fine wine on Zhongshan,
without being drunk for a thousand days.

Tea knives are a kind of tea utensil. According to the different tea utensils listed in writer Pi Rixiu's *Various Songs of Tea*, they are comprised of tea valley, tea server, tea sprouts, tea cabinet, tea room, tea oven, tea workshop, tea cauldron, tea cup, tea boiler, tea knife, etc.

Concerning the history of tea, the first composition that comes to mind is the tea sage of *The Classic of Tea*, Lu Yu. There is another writer from the same time period who was also fascinated with tea ceremony, Pi Rixiu. Pi Rixiu was a famous poet and writer of the late Tang Dynasty (618–907). With the equally famous Lu Guimeng, they were known together as "Pi Lu". Lu Xun once praised their essais of the late Tang Dynasty as being "the spearhead and splendor within a muddled and collapsing muddy pond".

Pi Rixiu became worthy of respect when he was young, but his official career was rough. His hobby during his early years was drinking. His poems were executed in an engrossing way. As such, he gave himself the nickname "Mr. Singing Drunk". When he was thirty-two years of age, Pi Rixiu was recommended by the state official to participate in the examinations in Chang'an. However, because he was not fond of officialdom, it was hard for him to accept the situation. Despite having talent, he had taken the examination several times before finally passing. What no one could have thought was the final obstacle hindering Pi Rixiu was his own appearance. Because the corner of his left eye was drooping, from a distance, he resembled what people called a "one-eyed person". His image was not good, nor did he like to find ways to get what he desired. As such, despite having spent a great deal of effort to pass the examination, he still merely served as a petty official from beginning to end. Pi Rixiu knew days where it was difficult to achieve his full ambition. He had resolutely sought asylum in the Huang Chao Peasant Uprising Army (875–884). In December 880 during the reign of Emperor Xi Zong, the volunteer army attacked Chang'an. Huang Chao was named emperor and Pi was appointed as member of Hanlin Imperial Academy. This was supposed as Pi Rixiu's highest state. Who would have known that he committed an offense against Huang Chao by writing a poem and was beheaded at once?

The aforementioned Boiling Tea, one of ten verses in *Various Songs of Tea* written by Pi Rixiu, describes tea being boiled. It expresses the author's fondness towards tea ceremony and the feeling of yearning for the country life. The line from the poem, "Drinking that fine wine on Zhongshan, without being drunk for a thousand days", does well to substitute wine for tea.

There are two Chinese scented rosewood tea knives — one is purple oil rosewood, and the other is dry rosewood. I am particularly fond of the purple oil rosewood. Several years ago, I obtained, from a friend in Hainan, a block of aged purple oil rosewood from the Bawang mountain range. It was in my possession for a time and I did not know what to do with it, at which point I gave it to a friend, Ren, in Beijing. After more than a year, I suddenly saw a purple oil rosewood tea knife from him. I was very fond of it. I knew I had to trouble Han from Shenyang to make another from that block of wood I had obtained long ago. I then gladly bought the item back and stored it on the shelf.

棋 罐

直径：12厘米　高7.5厘米　重：396.5克

题《八仙对弈图》（其二）

清·纪昀

局中局外两沉吟，犹是人间胜负心。
那似顽仙痴不省，春风蝴蝶睡乡深。

围棋起源于中国，早在春秋战国时期即有文献记载。隋唐时围棋经朝鲜传入日本，并流传到欧美各国。围棋蕴含着中华文化的丰富内涵，是中国文化与文明的体现。在古代，围棋一度是文人的专利，文人不齿于在围棋上一争胜负，而是把围棋当作一种文化，在黑白之间修身养性，忘却烦恼。围棋的黑白子、方棋盘形态，也蕴含着古代中国人的宇宙观。

此件海南黄花梨油梨围棋罐不仅器形端庄，而且成器已久，仍纹理清晰，荧光熠熠，开盖后降香浓郁。显然成器后并未被用作实用器，一直以文玩器被主人收藏。

黄花梨罐类文玩器的特别之处是内里不打磨，保持粗糙的表面接触空气，从而可使得黄花梨时刻散发降香。同时由于器物含盖子，降香就一直密封在罐内，一旦打开，便香气四溢，沁人心脾，让人上瘾，因此黄花梨文玩类罐器又得美名"品香罐"。此件器物为围棋罐，按说该是一对两只，或因原料不够，因此只成器一只，算是一点遗憾了，而残缺之美，也尤醉人心。

Jar for the Game of Go

Jar Diameter: 12 cm　　Height 7.5 cm　　Weight: 396.5 g

Written on the Painting "The Eight Immortals Playing the Game of Go"（2）
By Ji Yun of the Qing Dynasty

Those watching and those playing both ponder;
causing anxiety is the thought of victory and defeat.
It is a game, whether one is a celestial or imbecile.
If the outcome is unnerving, it is better to just sleep.

The game of Go originated from China. It was recorded in a document as early as the Spring and Autumn (770B.C.–476B.C.) and Warring States (475B.C.–221B.C.) periods. It was exported to Japan through Korea during the Sui (581–617) and Tang (618–907) Dynasties and had been circulated to European Countries. The game of Go is rich with meaning, as it reflects Chinese culture and civilization. During ancient times, the game of Go was once the possession of scholars. Scholars were unashamed to compete in Go. Rather, it was seen as a kind of culture, cultivating one's heart and character among the black and white pieces and forgetting one's worries. Go's black and white pieces and the square shape of the board also contains the world view held by Chinese people of ancient times.

This Hainan oily scented rosewood "Jar for the Game of Go" not only has a dignified form, but its fluorescent, glistening vein patterns are also distinct though it has been an exquisite piece for a long time. After opening the lid, it releases a rich rosewood fragrance. Clearly after it was made an exquisite piece and no longer used for practical purposes, the item has only been used for collection.

The special aspect of this rosewood scented jar-like collectable item lies in its unpolished interior. Once the preserved crude surface touches the air, the scented rosewood releases its fragrance. At the same time, since the object contains a lid, the rosewood scent can always be sealed up inside the jar. Once you open it, the aroma permeates the entire place, penetrating deep into the heart. It is mesmerizing, so the rosewood scented collectable jar-like object has also a good reputation for being an "aromatic jar". This object is a jar for the game of Go. Normally, it would be one of a pair. However, maybe due to the original material being insufficient, only one was made, which is a pity. As its beauty is incomplete, it is still fascinating.

立 柱

柱径：3.8 厘米　高：27.5 厘米　重：338.5 克

题西林壁

宋·苏轼

横看成岭侧成峰，远近高低各不同。
不识庐山真面目，只缘身在此山中。

　　这件黄花梨柱子是一截海南黄花梨糠梨老料标本。柱身通体布满 13 个鬼脸和鬼眼，纹理之间层峦叠嶂，是海黄多层纹理的标本料。

　　海南黄花梨的多层纹理十分特殊，不是单一虎皮纹或山水纹，而是几种纹理的相互交织。纹理间互相层叠，互相融合，错综复杂，给人别样的审美体验。在各种黄花梨相关文献中，至今我还没有发现这种情况的生成原因。但是我猜想，大致是由于黄花梨各个阶段的生长环境发生变化，抑或是营养基础发生改变，导致白皮转换成格的速度和过程不一，因此新的一层纹理盖着老的一层纹理出现。难以把握的美丽就连同观看者的思绪一起，像一层层的涟漪荡漾了开去。

Column

Tray Diameter: 3.8 cm　Height: 27.5 cm　Weight: 338.5 g

Inscribed on the Walls of Xilin Temple

By Su Shi of the Song Dynasty

In the front are mountain ranges; on the side are high summits; their distance and heights dissimilar.
Mt. Lushan's appearance cannot be distinguished, for I am on this mountain.

This scented rosewood column is from a section of dry, aged Chinese scented rosewood. The entire column shaft are covered in thirteen landscape-patterns and flecks, and there are many overlaps between the textures. It is a sample of Chinese scented rosewood layered wood veins.

The layered veins in Chinese scented rosewood is absolutely extraordinary. It not solely contains tiger-fur or mountain patterns, but rather several different patterns interweaving with

each other. The vein patterns are layered atop other patterns, mixing together into a complex entanglement, giving people a special kind of esthetic experience. I have not found out the cause for this kind of phenomenon discussed in documents about various kinds of scented rosewood till now. However, I suspect it is roughly due to the changes occuring in the environment during each stage of the scented rosewood's growth. It could also be due to the changes in its nutrition base, leading to differences in the transformation process and speed of the pith, resulting in a new layer of vein patterns emerging over the old layers. The beauty that is difficult to grasp and the observer's thoughts are like layers of ripples undulating together.

酒 瓶

瓶口径：4.5厘米　肚径：8.5厘米　高：15.5厘米　重：384.5克

饮中八仙歌（节选）
唐·杜甫

李白一斗诗百篇，长安市上酒家眠。
天子呼来不上船，自称臣是酒中仙。

北宋词人赵令畤曾在《侯鲭录》中记载："陶人之为器，有酒经焉……小颈、环口、修腹，受一斗，可以盛酒。"唐代诗人温庭筠曾在《乾䉉子·裴宏泰》中写道："（裴钧）有银海，受一斗以上，以手捧而饮。"所谓"酒经"与"银海"，都指酒瓶。"银海"即银质酒海，因此酒量很大的人，常被称之为"海量"。大凡嗜酒如命者，常常企盼着有一个酒海，使自己沉入酒海中，或者泛舟海上，时时畅饮。中国酒文化的历史源远流长，尤其是文坛士子，常常饮酒作诗，斗酒便有诗百篇，不胜枚举。诗与酒相从相随，几乎有一种天生的缘分。

此物件为酒瓶，按照古代酒瓶的形状所制，小口，溜肩，下腹较鼓，至底斜内收，小平底，整个造型挺拔俊秀。

此物件料质为中性料，油性和密度一般，但器型端庄比较漂亮，纹理也走位清晰，我作为中性料的标本而藏。

Wine Bottle

Bottle Mouth Diameter: 4.5 cm　Body Diameter: 8.5 cm　Height: 15.5 cm　Weight: 384.5 g

The Story of Eight Wine Bibbers（Excerpt）
By Du Fu of the Tang Dynasty

Li Bai can write hundreds of poems once he drinks several cups of wine.
When he gets drunk he sleeps in Chang'an City.
The emperor summoned him to write poems,
He rejected the emperor's demand and called himself an immortal of wine.

The poet, Zhao Lingzhi of the Northern Song Dynasty, wrote in his poem, *The Anecdotes and Novels of Houqing*: "A jiu jing made by potters can hold wine…It has a narrow neck, circular mouth, long body. It can hold one'dou' (about 2 liters) of wine." The poet, Wen

Tingyun from the Tang Dynasty, wrote in his poem *Qian Xun Zi – Pei Hongtai*, "If you have a 'yin hai', when drinking more than one mouth full, use both hands to drink." The so called "jiu jing" and "yin hai" both refer to a wine bottle. "Yin hai" (wine bottle, literally "silver sea"), also called 'yin zhi jiu hai' (wine bottle, literally "silver wine container"). As such, people with a great capacity for alcohol are often referred to as "hai liang" (literally "sea capacity"). Generally speaking, those who love wine as they love their life are often looking forward to having a "jiu hai", that is, a wine sea. They can submerse themselves in the sea of wine, or perhaps sail on top, often drinking to their heart's content. Chinese wine culture has a long flowing history, particularly when it comes to literary scholars, frequently drinking and composing poetry. Soon after indulging themselves in wine, their written verses would abound. Poetry and wine come hand in hand, almost like a natural fate.

This piece is a wine bottle made according to the shape of wine bottles in ancient times. It has a small mouth, sloped sides, a low, bulging belly slanting inwards towards the bottom, and a small, flat base. The entire model is tall and elegant.

The quality of the material of this object is neutral—the oiliness and density are ordinary. However, the modesty of its form is beautiful. The grain is also clear. I store it as a specimen of neutral quality.

仿古花瓶

瓶径：6厘米　高：12厘米　重：155.5克

瓶中梅（节选）
宋·曾几

小窗水冰青琉璃，梅花横斜三四枝。
若非风日不到处，何得色香如许时。

鲜花插瓶的兴盛发达是由宋代开始的，其影响欣赏趋势的重要因素是家具的变化，高坐家具的发展走向成熟，让精致的雅趣有了安顿之处。花瓶与家具恰逢其时地碰和，使鲜花插瓶顺应后者的需要而成为室内陈设的一部分。从传世绘画和考古墓室壁画来看，花瓶与同时发展起来的文房清玩共同构建起宋代士人书房与起居室布置的新格局，是生活中的艺术。

这件仿古花瓶是海黄老物件翻新抛光而成，大约成器在20世纪70年代。那个时代的海黄原料还都比较充足，因此会选择一些料质上乘的原料加工成工艺品，或出口创汇，或作为各种纪念品。

这件仿古花瓶经过了层层打磨，看得出历史的痕迹，同时也无须再深层打磨，其纹理已经全部体现。再打磨虽然能去掉些日晒雨淋造成的外层色差，但很可能会丢失很厚一层，得不偿失。所以主人保持了现在这个状态，我觉得非常合适。

从纹理看，此花瓶有典型的两层纹理，外面一层像涟漪一样，在一个鬼脸周围层层散开；里面还包融了一层如旭日东升，从上往下发散如光芒般的黑色线条，煞是美妙。

Pseudo-Classical Vase

Vase Diameter: 6 cm　Height: 12 cm　Weight: 155.5 g

Plum Flowers in the Vase(Excerpt)
By Zeng Ji of the Song Dynasty

Ice covers the green colored glass; plum blossoms cover the few slanting branches.
If it weren't for the wind and sunshine, I would not be able to appreciate the view.

Displaying flowers in vases has been popular since the Song Dynasty. The change in furniture is the important factor that influenced this trend of aesthetics. Development towards tall pieces of furniture matured, making a place for exquisite and

elegant articles. The flower vase and furniture met at just the right time. Putting flowers in a vase adapted to the needs of the latter, becoming a part of the indoor display. Paintings passed down from ancient times, murals from archaeological burial chambers, and flower vases together with the simultaneously developing appreciation of stationary objects constructed a new arrangement for the layout of the studio of Song Dynasty scholars. This is art in daily life.

This pseudo-classical flower vase was refurbished and polished from an old Chinese scented rosewood object. It was made in 1970s. At that time, Chinese scented rosewood material was still comparatively abundant. As such, some first-rate material could still be selected to be processed into a handicraft, to be exported to a foreign country, or to be used as any kind of souvenir.

This pseudo-classical flower vase has passed through layers upon layers of polishing. You can see its trace through history. At the same time, it won't ever experience another deep layer of polishing. Its veins are already reflected in its entirety. Although polishing it again could get rid of some color inferiority of the outer layer brought about by weathering, it would probably lose a very thick layer. The benefits would not make up for the loss. Therefore, the owner has maintained its current condition, which I think is very suitable.

The wood grain of this flower vase has two typical layers of veins. The outer layer resembles ripples. Layer upon layers spread out around the spider-webbing pattern. The inside contains a layer like the rising sun ascending in the east. The top layers' black lines are like extremely beautiful rays of light being dispersed downward.

木 枕

长：19.5厘米　宽：7厘米　高：5厘米　重：580.5克

浣溪沙·几共查梨到雪霜
宋·苏轼

几共查梨到雪霜，一经题品便生光，木奴何处避雌黄。
北客有来初未识，南金无价喜新尝，含滋嚼句齿牙香。

古人的枕头多为硬物，主要的一点是为了凉快。因人在入睡后，尤其夏天，头部的温度会升高，古代没有高科技来降温，睡硬枕则具有清凉、去热的物理性能，他们便是用这种简单实在的办法来帮助自己入睡。

从"枕"字的造字上来看，最初做枕头的材料或许就是木头。确实在汉代以前，古人多用木枕或石枕。至战国时期，枕头已经相当讲究。在河南信阳的一个战国楚墓里，出土了一张保存完好的漆木床，床上有竹枕。至宋代，瓷枕进入发展繁荣期，不仅器形较前代有所增大，而且装饰技法也突飞猛进，刻、划、剔、印、堆塑等技法纷纷被采用，极大地丰富了枕头的表现力和艺术性。枕头在古代不仅体现了主人的品位，制枕用贵材也是身份与地位的象征。玉枕被古人视为珍宝，多为皇帝的御用品。

同样的，海南黄花梨作为珍贵的木材也一直受文人墨客与达官显贵的喜爱。明清时期，皇家也斥巨资采购黄花梨制器。

海黄木料做枕，加工性能良好，软硬轻重适中，不易变形，色泽柔和，加上海黄香味让人上瘾，枕之入睡，其梦也醉。

Wood Pillow

Length: 19.5 cm　Width: 7 cm　Height: 5 cm　Weight: 580.5 g

Washing Silk in the Creek - Unlike Hawthorns and Pears, Orange Trees Rarely Remain Green in the Frost Season
By Su Shi of the Song Dynasty

Unlike hawthorns and pears, orange trees rarely remain green in the frost season.
The comments and odes to oranges made them special.
Where can oranges avoid being talked about?
I did not know orange trees when I first came to Huangzhou.
What I knew was oranges were dramatically expensive in the south and I was willing to have a taste.
Having a good taste of an orange while writing orange-themed poetry,
I feel that both my mouth and my poetry are full of orange fragrance.

Pillows of ancient times were often hard, mainly to keep one cool. After one has fallen asleep, especially during summer time, the temperature of one's head can rise. People of ancient times didn't have high tech to make them cooler. Instead, sleeping on a hard pillow would cool them down. It had the physical function of eliminating the heat. They would use this precise, simple method to help them fall asleep.

The Chinese character for pillow is "枕" ("zhen"). The first material used to make a pillow was possibly wood ("wood" being "木" ("mu") as seen in the character "枕"). In fact, before the Han Dynasty (206B.C.–220A.D.), people used wooden or stone pillows. During the Warring States Period, the pillow was already being carefully considered. In a grave site of Chu kingdom in Warring States Period in Xinyang, Henan Province, an intact, conserved lacquer wooden bed was dug up. On top of the bed was a bamboo pillow. In the Song Dynasty, porcelain pillows entered into a time of prosperous development. Not only was it somewhat bigger than those of the previous generation, but the decorative techniques had also advanced by leaps and bounds. Such techniques as carving, inscribing, engraving, stamping, and layering, were adopted one after the other, enriching pillows' expressive power greatly. Pillows in ancient times not only reflected the owner's tastes, but the expensive material used was also a symbol of the owner's identity and status. People from ancient times viewed jade pillows as a treasure and it was more often used by the emperor.

Similarity, scholars and high-ranking officials and dignitaries were also fond of the precious Chinese scented rosewood. During the Ming and Qing Dynasties, the imperial household vastly expanded the purchasing of scented rosewood items.

The processability of scented rosewood to make pillows is good; the severity of its hardness is moderate, and it does not tend to deform. The color and luster is gentle and adding a little scented rosewood aroma is mesmerizing. Falling asleep on this pillow gives one enchanting dreams.

擀面杖

长：35厘米　头径：2.5厘米　腰径：5厘米　重：430克

同儿辈赋未开海棠
元·元好问

枝间新绿一重重，小蕾深藏数点红。
爱惜芳心莫轻吐，且教桃李闹春风。

海南黄花梨非常珍贵，历史上收藏或使用的阶层非富即贵。改革开放后，随着经济的快速发展，中国赏玩黄花梨的群体也迅速扩大。但黄花梨由于本身成材慢，加上产地和数量十分稀少，可想而知，根本无法满足市场需要，因此便出现了几个现象：首先是价格疯涨，木材居然到了论克卖的境地；其次是为了材料挖地三尺，把当年黄花梨砍伐后留在山里的树根都挖出来；最后便是把民间，主要是黎族人日常实用的黄花梨器具都淘出来当宝。我刚入门的时候，也是疯狂爱上黎族民俗老物件，花了大价钱收了很多黄花梨刨子、织刀等，这件擀面杖就是那时候收到的。

这件擀面杖是由糠梨干料所制，打磨至5000目后荧光闪闪，通体遍布十多个鬼眼鬼脸，材质细腻不见棕眼，表面有浅浅的蟹爪纹，是标准海南黄花梨老物件的纹理。

其实黎族的海黄实用器具是不少的，但是最后流通到市面上完整的东西却不多。一方面，是被一些中意民俗物件的藏家收起来了；另一方面，也是更主要的原因，便是无知的商家都拿去车了珠子。海黄手串最风行的时候，商家每天满世界找原料做珠子。民俗老物件料多，且年份久远，质地优良，因此经常会开出诸如紫油梨对眼等极品的手串。如果运气好，小几千的料子，成品便是大几万的手串。手串是整个海黄文玩圈流通最快的物件，因此对追求现金流的商家来说，没有比做手串更有吸引力的事情了。况且也有大部分老物件因年代久远，表面坑洼，风吹虫咬，很难看出里面的真实质地。卖家又不肯打磨干净，因为一打磨，分量就去掉很多，所以多是开一个小窗，甚至都不给开窗，全凭买家眼力。因此，民俗老物件做珠子，变成一个赌料加快速变现的生意，深得商人欢心。

但我始终觉得，海黄老物件最大的意义，是传承。能让接手的人欣赏海黄纹理之美的同时，了解物件原来的用处，体会黎族人生活的点滴，才是海黄老物文玩的真正打开方式。

Rolling Pin

Length: 35 cm　Head Diameter: 2.5 cm　Middle Diameter: 5 cm　Weight: 430 g

Composing a Poem for the Begonia in Bud
By Yuan Haowen of the Yuan Dynasty

There are green sprouts among the branches while buds wait to flourish.
It would be better to refrain your tender care from display,
letting other flowers compete for the most glamorous in spring.

Chinese scented rosewood is extremely precious. The class that collected or used them in history was either rich or noble. After reform and opening-up, and the fast development of China's economy, more and more people began to collect and enjoy the scented rosewood items. However, due to scented rosewood's maturing slowly and there being few sources, its quantity is very sparse. As one can imagine, the marketplace's demands simply cannot be satisfied. As such, a few phenomenon have arisen. First, prices are insanely high. Wood is now unexpectedly sold in grams. Second, to dig the material out. The tree roots of the cut down scented rosewood left in the mountains are all dug out. And finally, the scented rosewood utensils used daily by the Li ethnic people are all seen as treasures. When I started my collections, I was in crazy love with the old objects of the Li ethnic people's popular custom. I spent tons of money on many scented rosewood planes, knives, etc. This rolling pin was received precisely at that time.

This rolling pin was made from dry scented rosewood. After using a sandpaper grain of 5,000 grit to polish it, it became fluorescent and glistening. The entire pin is covered densely with more than ten landscape wood grain patterns. The texture of the wood is exquisite and no flecks are seen. The surface has very shallow crab claw wood grain lines, typical of Chinese scented rosewood.

In fact, there are many Chinese scented rosewood utensils used by the Li ethnic people. However, there are not many complete items that have circulated to the market. On one hand, some have been taken by collectors. On the other hand, ignorant merchants turned them into beads, which is the main cause When Chinese scented rosewood bracelets were most fashionable, merchants went everywhere to find materials to make beads. There was a lot of materials from old traditional objects. They were quiet aged and the texture was first-rate. As such, you could frequently see bracelets of the best quality purple oil scented rosewood. If you were in luck, a small piece of material could turn into bracelets worthy tens of thousands yuan. Bracelets were the quickest to circulate within the Chinese scented rosewood collector's item circle. As such, there was nothing more attractive to merchants who pursue the cash flow than bracelets. Moreover, most old objects, have a dip in the surface and have been exposed to the wind and insects, so it is difficult to see its true texture. Sellers won't agree to have it polished clean either. Once it is polished, it loses a lot of weight. Therefore, many sellers allow just a small section to be cut to examine the quality or they don't allow it to be cut at all. It all comes down to the buyer's perspective. As such, making old traditional objects into beads became the drive for betting on material to accelerate sales, which was deeply favored by merchants.

However, I always thought being able to pass on Chinese scented rosewood items was most meaningful, letting people appreciate the beauty of the wood grain patterns and, at the same time, understand the object's original function. This is the right way to deal with Chinese scented rosewood collector's items.

文 盒

长：20.5 厘米　　宽：13.5 厘米　　高：6.5 厘米　　重（一对）：882 克

福建仙游榜头镇是中国红木家具主要集散地。在这里，黄花梨的原料存量甚至超过海南原产地，几乎所有黄花梨商家和文玩爱好者都把此地看作圣地。几年前我和两位友人也去"朝圣"了一次。因为时值春节假期，开门的商家很少，但是仍然在少数开门的商家中看到了无数令人着迷甚至惊叹的海黄文玩和家具，小至手串把件，大至罗汉床、顶箱柜，应有尽有，令人大开眼界。

这对文盒就是那次仙游之旅带回来的。文盒一对两只，面板由一块非常绚丽的老料对开而成，因此成器后两盒完全对称，甚是漂亮。文盒表面高抛打磨至 5000 目以上，而内里不打磨，因为文盒除了作为装载物件的实用器，还有另一独特的使用功能，就是闻香。

黄花梨又称"降香黄檀"，是一种珍贵的药材，它的香味是除了黄花梨绚丽花纹外另一个让人着迷的地方。这种香味人们通常称之为"降香"，人们也把是否有降香作为真假黄花梨的判断依据。当然，黄花梨紫油梨和糠梨、新料和老料、根料和枝料、越黄和海黄，香味都有所不同，因此也不能一概而论。拿香味作为评判黄花梨的标准，只可当作参考。

文盒，作为一种实用型文玩器具，是经过很长时间，一步步从古到今演进而生的。具体要从最早的庋具[1]讲起。在夏商周及以前，庋具是一种贮藏用家具，供存储衣物。战国庋具主要是箱，使用木材或竹材制作，早期由两块实木凿成，上下扣在一起。秦汉庋具仍以箱为主。汉代木箱普遍为平顶式和盝顶式。除箱外，汉代又出现木柜、木橱和竹材编织的笥。隋唐五代时期，南方庋具多用竹材，如笥、橱、箱、笼；北方多用木材，如箱、柜、匣、椟。因选材不同，加工工艺不同，造型也有差异。隋唐时期，庋具的用途就不单是存储衣物，也用来收纳书画、饭食、钱币等。两宋时期，箱、柜、橱等传统庋具的结构比唐代更简洁、更适用，如增加了抽屉。这个阶段古人对收纳贮藏的要求已经越来越高，家具上也有了细分的应用。

至明清两代，中国传统家具的发展达到高峰。家具制作更侧重于微观，审美趣味转向精细工巧、繁丽富缛，工艺技术方面也发展到历史上从未有过的高度。这个阶段的庋具，有小型庋具、箱、格、圆角柜、方角柜和闷户柜几种。小型庋具体量小，制作精巧，置于桌案之上，如存入化妆品的"头面匣"、存放金银首饰的"百宝箱"、放置贵重药品的"小药箱"，诸凡奁、匣、盒或小型的箱都可归属于此。现在的文盒，也是归属于此。

起初文盒专门用于存放收纳各种文房用具，以实用为主，便于出行使用，后逐渐发展为以收藏与鉴赏为主的艺术珍玩。由于里面所藏都是主人珍爱之物，而黄花梨本身又是极为珍贵的材料，因此黄花梨的文盒便也成为文玩市场的宠爱之物。

---

[1] 庋（guǐ）具，用来贮藏物品的家具，如箱、柜、橱类。

Boxes

Length: 20.5 cm   Width: 13.5 cm   Height: 6.5 cm   Total Weight (a pair): 882 g

Bangtou Town in Xianyou County, Putian, Fujian Province is a major Chinese distribution center of mahogany furniture. The amount of scented rosewood in reserve here exceeds even that of the original source. Almost all merchants and collectors of scented rosewood see this place as the holy city. Some years ago, two friends and I "made pilgrimage" to this place once. Because it happened to be the Spring Festival at that time, not many shops were open. However, there were still a small number of shops open and they had attractive Chinese scented rosewood collector's items and furniture that were captivating and surprising to countless people. From small items like bead bracelets to Luohan beds and cabinets, everything you could think of was there. It was eye opening.

This pair of boxes was precisely what I brought back from my trip to Xianyou. The face of the box is made from a block of gorgeous, aged material. They are made symmetrically. It is extremely beautiful. The surface of the box was polished at high speed, using more than 5,000 grade sandpaper grit. The inside was not polished, because other than being used to carry items, it has an additional, unique function—its fragrance.

Scented rosewood is also called fragrant rosewood. It is a kind of precious ingredient for medicine. Besides the scented rosewood's gorgeous patterns, its fragrance is also fascinating. People often call this aroma "jiang xiang" (literally "descending fragrance"). They judge whether scented rosewood is fake or genuine based on whether or not it has that "descending fragrance". Of course, the aroma of purple oil and dry scented rosewood, new and old wood, wood from the roots and wood from branches, Vietnamese and Chinese scented rosewood all differ to some extent. Thus, as different matters cannot be lumped together, the aroma cannot be used as the standard to judge scented rosewood. It can be only used as a reference.

The box is a kind of practical collector's item. It has evolved step by step since ancient times. It evolved specifically from the earliest wardrobe. During the Xia, Shang, and Zhou Dynasties (the earliest named dynasties) and earlier, the box was a kind of furniture used for storage, mainly for clothing. In the Warring States Period, wardrobe was a box made of wood or bamboo. During early periods, two blocks of wood were chiseled and fastened together.

In Qin and Han Dynasties wardrobes were mainly boxes. In Han Dynasty wooden boxes generally had a flat or box top. Aside from the box, wooden wardobes again appeared during the Han Dynasty. The wooden wardrobe was a container weaved with bamboo. During the Sui, Tang, and Five Dynasties, the boxes in the south were made of bamboo and could be used as a container (a wardrobe, chest, or basket) for food or clothing. In the north, they were made of wood and could be made into a chest, wardrobe, small box, or case. They were made and shaped according to the different materials used. Wardrobes of the Sui and Tang Dynasties (581–617 and 618–907 respectively) were not only used to store clothing, but also paintings, calligraphy, food, money, etc. During the Song Dynasty (960–1279), the structure of chests, wardrobes, cabinets, and such wardrobes were more concise and applicable (having added drawers) compared to the Tang Dynasty. At this stage, the requirements of people from ancient times towards storage were already increasing. Furniture also had a subdivision of use.

During the Ming and Qing Dynasties, Chinese traditional furniture reached the peak of development. A particular emphasis was placed on small esthetics and more meticulous designs. They were richly adorned, complicated, and beautiful. The technological aspect of art also developed to a height never seen before in history. The boxes, at this stage, consisted of small scale cupboards, chests, frames, and wardrobes with round or square angles, sealed wardrobes, and a variety of designs. The capacity of some of the boxes was small. They were elaborate, placed on the table and used as "head-ornament cases" for storing cosmetics, "jewelry boxes" for storing gold and silver jewelry, "small medicine boxes" for storing precious medicine. Now, the collectable boxes also belong to this category.

Originally, collectable boxes were used by specialists to store collectable utensils. Relying on its practicality, it was easy to use during travel. Afterwards, it gradually developed into a precious collectable piece of art for storage or for the appreciation of the viewer. Due to the stored items being things cherished by its owner and scented rosewood itself being extremely precious as well, scented rosewood boxes have become a collector's item to dote on in the marketplace.

帽 筒

筒高：23.2厘米　筒口直径：8.4厘米　肚径：8.1厘米
底面直径：7.2厘米　顶端开孔直径：3厘米　深：8.2厘米　重：1 018克

　　帽筒是以前用来摆放帽子的器物。古代官员退朝回府和从官署返家，须更衣脱帽。由于帽子有帽翅和花翎，故要用特别的托架摆放。帽架和帽筒也因此成为官员家居必备之物。

　　清人李兆洛（1769—1841）的《帽筒铭》称赞帽筒"头容之直骨所植，庄诚劲正思比德。崔巍切云惟女克，冠圆象天知天时。寒暑一节能者谁，虽在闲处宜得师。"帽筒令帽子笔直，使人仪容端正；帽筒本身直立笔挺，有庄诚劲正之德，虽身形高耸，仿佛与云天相接，不过最后也为人所用，使帽子不受寒暑所侵。帽筒挂上圆帽后，形态犹如天穹，展现顺天应时之理。故虽为小物，却有教人师法之处。

　　此帽筒几年前从一位无锡藏友手中获得，是本人尤为喜爱的一件海南黄花梨老物件，为海南黄花梨黄梨圆木老料而制，一木而成。筒身圆直，外观圆润，素净无饰，工型俱佳。弦面柔和荧光性强，麦穗纹特征明显，纹理呈现典型的行云流水纹，亦如国画之山水水墨画卷。树结如一轮圆日照耀大地，峰峦逶迤叠嶂，一气呵成。亦有20多个小鬼眼忽隐忽现。

　　此物件材质细腻，轻抚如丝绸般柔滑，手感压手，降香味醇正。原被用作达官贵人的帽筒，但料想实际使用不多，成器后多半直接被用作案头雅器，供观赏把玩之用。

Hat Stand

Stand Height: 23.2 cm　Diameter of the Stand's Mouth: 8.4 cm　Belly Diameter: 8.1 cm
Base Diameter: 7.2 cm　Interior Diameter: 3 cm　Depth: 8.2 cm　Weight: 1,018 g

The hat stand once used to arrange hats. During ancient times, officials going to work and returning home from the official institution would need to change clothes and remove their hats. Due to hats having wings and plumes, a special bracket was needed. A hat rack and hat stand thus became an essential in the homes of officials.

Li Zhaoluo (1769–1841) of the Qing Dynasty complimented the hat stands in his *Inscriptions of Hat Stands*, "The hat is stored in good shape because it is put on a cylinder hat stand. The hat stand itself is upright, representing uprightness and morality. High and lofty, the hat stand seems to reach into the sky. The round shape of the hat is like the sky from which we determine the time and season. The hat stand helps store hats and protect them from the effects brought about by changing seasons. Normal as the cylinder hat stand is, we can learn a lot from it." He believed hat stands kept hats straight, causing people to appear upright. Hat stand are very straight and erect. It has a character of being honest, strong, and upright. Although its form stands tall, it's as though it interlocks with the

clouds in the sky. However, they were at last used to protect hats from the heat and cold. After hats were hung on the stand, its form was like a vault of heaven, displaying a timely, heavenly order. Although it is a small object, it has something for people to learn.

This hat stand was received from a friend in Wuxi years ago. It was an aged Chinese scented rosewood piece I was especially fond of. It was made from a round piece of Chinese scented rosewood. The item has a cylindicular, straight body. The exterior is smooth and round. Its nature is calm and unadorned and its workmanship is excellent. Its tangential surface is gentle with a strong fluorescence. Its characteristic wheat-patterned wood grain is distinct. The vein lines demonstrate a typical natural and unforced pattern. It also resembles a Chinese ink and wash painting of a mountains and rivers landscape. The knot in the wood is like a round sun shining brightly on the earth with a high mountain range winding, folding, and flowing smoothly over a range of peaks. There are over twenty small flecks appearing clearly around the item.

This object's material is exquisite. The feel of the surface is as smooth and soft as silk and the rosewood scent is pure. The hat stand was originally used by high officials and noble persons. In reality, however, it was not used often. After it came into development, it was used more often as an ornament to decorate one's desk.

虎皮纹花瓶

高：19.8 厘米　瓶口直径：8.7 厘米　肚径：8.4 厘米　底面直径：8.1 厘米
花瓶开孔直径：3 厘米　深：13.5 厘米　重：524 克

此物件为海南黄花梨老物件翻新打磨而成，是20世纪70年代末的老工艺品。当时，海南省各地工艺品厂以当地特产海南黄花梨木为材料，生产了一大批各式各样的民俗工艺品，从杯、盘、碗、罐，到算盘、闹钟、台灯等，五花八门，应有尽有。那时的中国刚进入改革开放初期，工艺品厂还都是国营体制，产品大多以生活用品为原型，外观简朴、结实耐用。琼山县的算盘、火车头牌的闹钟，都是当时的明星产品。另外，为争取出口创汇，销往海外的海黄工艺品，个个选料上乘、做工精良，受到国外市场的普遍欢迎。我藏有一副海南黄花梨的老工艺品算盘，上面的标签都是直接用美元标注的。后来，由于国企改制，同时海南黄花梨原料急剧减少，这些存世的物件都慢慢散入民间。由于这些物件的制作都极为费工费料，如今，再也不会有任何商家和玩家会用黄花梨原料来制作相同的物件了，因此这些老工艺品就成为海南黄花梨文玩市场的孤品，较为珍贵。

此海南黄花梨花瓶外观圆润，工型俱佳。表面品相完整，轻抚表面手感如丝绸般柔滑，瓶口有一处树结。材质细腻几乎不见毛孔，麦穗纹特征明显纹理清晰，表面虎皮纹理呈现典型的山水纹，瓶口带有发散剖面鬼眼，瓶身7个大小鬼眼忽隐忽现，弦面柔和荧光性强。

此物适合闲暇时用作禅房及博古架上的装饰摆件，观时赏心悦目，玩时豪情逸致，实乃让人喜不自胜。

Tiger Fur-Patterned Flower Vase

Height: 19.8 cm　Vase Mouth Lip Diameter: 8.7 cm　Belly Diameter: 8.4 cm　Base Diameter: 8.1 cm
Vase Mouth Interior Diameter: 3 cm　Depth: 13.5 cm　Weight: 524 g

This vase was refurbished and polished from an aged object made of Chinese scented rosewood. It is an old handiwork from the end of the 1970s. At that time, handicraft factories of various regions in Hainan used local scented rosewood, producing large quantities of all kinds of items related to popular customs, from cups, dishes, bowls, and pots to abaci, alarm clocks, table lamps, and a myriad of items you could ever need. China, at that time, had just entered into the initial stage of reform and opening up. Handicraft factories were still a part of the state-run system. For the most part, goods were modeled after articles used for daily life. Their appearance was simple, unadorned, and quite durable. The Qiongshan County abacus and the Locomotive (Huo Che Tou) brand alarm clock were both star products of that time. In addition, in order to strive to export to foreign countries and receive widespread approval of foreign markets, scented rosewood crafts sold overseas are made of first-rate material and excellent workmanship. I have collected an old set of Chinese scented rosewood handcrafted abacuses. The tag on top is marked directly in U.S. dollars. Afterwards, due to the state enterprise changing systems and the amount of Chinese scented rosewood material having decreased rapidly, the remaining articles were slowly dispersed among the people. Due to the manufacturing of these articles being extremely laborious and material consuming, merchants and enthusiasts now no longer use scented rosewood to manufacture the same object. Consequently, these old, fairly precious crafts have become a lone rosewood scented collectable item in the marketplace.

This Chinese scented rosewood flower vase has a smooth and round exterior, an excellent model of workmanship. The condition of the surface is complete. Stroking the surface feels as soft and smooth as silk. A tree knot is located at the vase's mouth. The texture is exquisite with hardly any pores visible. The characteristic wheat lines are clear and the vein lines distinct. The tiger fur—patterned veins demonstrate a model of natural veins - like moving clouds and flowing water. Flecks are dispersed in sections around the vase's mouth. Seven flecks of various sizes appear clearly on the vase's body. The vertical section is soft and has a strong fluorescense.

When not in use, the object is suitable to be arranged for decoration in a meditation abode or atop antique shelves. It's pleasing to the eye and gives you an incredible joy—a grand, carefree feeling when handled.

山水随形

长：22 厘米　宽：24 厘米　高：65 厘米　重：3 500 克

这件紫油梨《山水随形》尺寸较大，如一座巍峨山峰，中间山窟洞开，令人想到天门山之景象，颇为神奇。整件作品置于一个黑檀底座之上，威武大气。料质油性十足，棕眼全无，轻轻擦拭后表面泛出晶莹的光泽，是紫油梨中的上品。

这里要聊到一个海南黄花梨成材的特殊过程：虫蚀。海南黄花梨成材需要三五百年，成材后才可以砍伐做家具。但是，新砍伐后的黄花梨是不能立即使用的，必须经过三至五年的自然风化虫蚀的过程。早先，黎族百姓砍完黄花梨树木后会先将树木原地卧倒静置，而不是直接外运出售。因为黄花梨真正有用的只有中间的"格"，周围白皮没用且湿，因此木材极重，砍削白皮费时费力，所以索性先放着。而后，黄花梨边材部分为淡黄色无气味的软质体，最受白蚁青睐。所以白蚁遇到了砍伐后的黄花梨后，会在一到三年时间内将边材部分咬蚀，至遇到有辛辣芳香而又坚硬的心材部分时自然停止。可用的黄花梨心材部分就这样保留了下来。

《广东新语·卷二十四·虫语·白蚁》："广多白蚁，以卑湿而生，凡物皆食。虽金、银至坚亦食，唯不能食铁力木与棕木耳。然金、银虽食，以其渣滓煎之，复为金银，金银之性不变也。性不变则质也不变。铁力，金之木也。木中有金，金为木质，故也不能损。"在黄花梨的虫蚀过程中，白蚁成了名副其实的义工，不需黎族百姓人工动斧头了。

在这三年左右的虫蚀时间内，干湿季节不断转换，黄花梨心材也直接经过了反复多次的干燥、潮化，部分颜色趋于加深，醇厚而均匀，油质及芳香物质浸润全身，使其玉质感更加鲜明。

这极为耗费时间的虫蚀过程也是海黄更为珍贵的原因之一。一棵百年的海黄树，砍伐后经过虫蚀过程，最后剩下的可能只有原来的四分之一，甚至更少。这件紫油梨随形的形成，就是一截黄花梨在野外经过风吹雨淋、虫蚀鼠咬后自然而成。观之，可知海黄成才不易；赏之，可得海黄随形之美。

Naturally Form

Length: 22 cm　Width: 24 cm　Height: 65 cm　Weight: 3,500 g

The size of this purple oil scented rosewood "Naturally Form" is rather large. It is like towering mountain peaks. In between the mountains are wide open caves. It causes people to think of the Tianmen Mountain scene, which is quite magical. The entire piece was placed on a dark sandalwood base, giving it a formidable atmosphere. The quality of the oiliness is ample. There are absolutely no flecks in the wood grain. After lightly wiping the surface, the luster sparkles and is translucent. It is a product of high grade purple oil scented rosewood.

Below we talk about a special process concerning Chinese scented rosewood: erosion by insects. For Chinese scented rosewood to become usable, it required several hundred years. Afterwards, it can be cut down and made into furniture. However, newly cut down Chinese scented rosewood cannot be used immediately. It must undergo three to five years of a natural process where insects eat the wood. Before, after the Li ethnic people finished chopping the scented rosewood trees, they would leave the trees lying down where they were chopped, and not directly ship them off to be sold, because the truly useful portion of scented rosewood lies on the inside—the "ge", or pith. The surrounding bark is moist and useless. Therefore, since the wood is extremely heavy and paring the bark takes time and great effort, you might as well first let it sit. Afterwards, the sapwood portion becomes soft, odorless, and turns a light yellow. At this point, it is most favorable to termites. As such, the termites take one to three years to tear down the scented rosewood. Once the pith becomes hard and the aroma biting, they naturally cease. The usable portion of the scented rosewood is retained this way.

New Dialect of Guangdong - Volume 24 - Insect Dialect- Termites writes, "Termites are numerous and like to chew on things. They eat everything, even gold and silver despite being hard. The only thing they do not eat is ironwood and long tree fungus. Although they eat gold and silver, you can refine its excrement and it will return to its original form. Its nature and quality do not change. Ironwood is the gold of wood. Gold is in the wood and the wood is gold. It cannot be harmed." In the process of insects eating the scented rosewood, termites have become volunteer workers, not just in name. Li workers do not need to move an axe.

Around the three years of being eaten by insects, the dry and humid seasons change ceaselessly. The pith of the scented rosewood passes through many drying and moistening cycles. Part of the color will tend to darken, becoming evenly mellow and rich. The oiliness and fragrant substance will permeate through the whole body, making its jade-like feel more distinct.

This extremely time consuming process of being eaten by insects is one of the reasons that cause Chinese scented rosewood to be even more precious. The remainder of a hundred-year-old Chinese scented rosewood tree which has been chopped down and undergone the process is probably a quarter of the original or even less. This purple oil scented rosewood item's shape was formed naturally. That is, the shape of the chunk of scented rosewood in the countryside was formed from the wind and rain and insects and rats. If you observe closely, it is evident it was not easy for this Chinese scented rosewood to become this way and you can appreciate the natural beauty of this Chinese scented rosewood.

水波纹盘

盘径：21 厘米　高：2.5 厘米　重：314.5 克

望洞庭
唐·刘禹锡

湖光秋月两相和，潭面无风镜未磨。
遥望洞庭山水翠，白银盘里一青螺。

越南黄花梨，大约从 1996 年以后出现在市场上，其心材、边材区别明显，边材浅黄色，心材浅黄、黄及红褐色至深褐色，夹带有深色条纹，具有酸香味。

越黄与海黄两者长在气候相同、地理相近的同纬度地区，材质、纹理、香气很接近。大部分好辨识，但有些则到了比孙悟空与六耳猕猴还难分辨，愣是观世音菩萨也被难倒的地步。总结起来，越黄与海黄大约有以下几点比较明显的不同：一是相对而言，海黄纹理（棕眼）细，越黄纹理粗一些。二是越黄香味略小，新切面有较浓的酸香气味；海黄味道则浓郁一些，即所说的"降香"，最初切面有种刺鼻的辛辣味，放置一段时间之后，慢慢地有降香出现。三是海黄纹理好，鬼脸多，越黄相对差一些。四是颜色上二者也有区别，海黄颜色深一些，越黄浅一些。五是从材料上看，越黄树材粗大，海黄树材直径普遍较小，现在见到的越南黄花梨心材直径大多在 20～40 厘米。

Ripple-Patterned Tray

Tray Diameter: 21 cm   Height: 2.5 cm   Weight: 314.5 g

Since 1996, Vietnamese scented rosewood has appeared in the marketplace. The difference between its pith and sapwood is distinct: the sapwood is a pale yellow; the pith is a light yellow, yellow and reddish brown to dark brown with dark brown veins. It has a sour fragrance.

Vietnamese scented rosewood and Chinese scented rosewood both grow in the same climate. As these trees are found in similar geography on the same latitude, the quality, wood grain, and fragrance are quite similar. Most are distinguishable, and yet, some are more difficult to distinguish than the Monkey King and the Six-eared Macaque. Guanyin, the Bodhisattva of Compassion, unexpectedly, has also been stumped. To summarize, the following points out the rather obvious differences. First, comparatively speaking, the veins (flecks) in Chinese scented rosewood are thin, while the veins in Vietnamese scented rosewood are thicker. Second, the fragrance of Vietnamese scented rosewood is quite subtle. A newly cut section has a relatively strong, tart fragrance; the aroma of the Chinese scented rosewood is stronger. The widely called "rosewood" when first cut has a kind of acrid, pungent aroma. After it sits for a while, the rosewood fragrance slowly emerges. Third, the veins of Chinese scented rosewood are better, the "spider-webbing" grain patterns are more numerous, while those of the Vietnamese scented rosewood are poorer. Fourth, they differ in color: the tint of the Chinese scented rosewood is deeper while that of the Vietnamese scented rosewood is paler. Fifth, in terms of material, Vietnamese scented rosewood is thicker; the diameter of Chinese scented rosewood, in general, tends to be smaller. The pith's diameter of the Vietnamese scented rosewood seen today tends to be between 20~40 centimeters.

镇 纸

长：7.7厘米　宽：4.1厘米　高：1.5厘米　重：105.8克

镇纸，是放置在书桌案头上的文房用品，顾名思义，即指写字作画时用以压纸的东西，现今常见的多为长方条形，因故也称作"镇尺""压尺"。有的成对，有的单件，单件的即称"单镇"。镇纸正式进入书房不晚于南北朝，《南史·垣荣祖传》中记："帝尝以书案下安鼻为盾，以铁为书镇，如意甚壮大，以备不虞，欲以代杖。"由此可见，镇纸至今已有逾1500年历史。

文献中对镇纸多有论及。唐杜光庭《录异记·异石》中记："会稽进士李眺，偶拾得小石，青黑平正，温滑可玩，用为书镇焉。"宋张镃诗云："三山放翁实赠我，镇纸恰称金犀牛。"明顾清诗云："文木裁成体直方，高斋时伴校书郎。"宋元及以前的镇纸甚少有传世品。明代镇纸，其形多为尺状，上有兽钮，与文献记载相符，如铜虎钮镇纸，长方尺形底座，上有蹲虎一头，虎头雕工细腻写实，虎尾写意粗犷。

清代铜镇纸在沿袭明代风格的同时有所创新，特别是随着工艺技术的进步，装饰味道十分浓郁的镇纸开始出现，可谓集观赏性与实用性于一器。

镇纸既可作为实用器，也可作为文玩件。在当今的文玩圈内，以紫檀和黄花梨为料做成的镇纸是流行主体。

这把镇纸原是一块满水波纹的海南黄花梨家具料，纹理清晰，油性出众，后修整成为一把极其出众的文玩押方镇纸。

Paperweight

Length: 7.7 cm　　Width: 4.1 cm　　Height: 1.5 cm　　Weight: 105.8 g

The paperweight is a collector's item that can be placed on one's desk. The paperweight, as the name implies, was used to press paper down, mainly while writing characters or painting. Now, paperweights are commonly long and rectangular, and some come in pairs. The single ones are called "danzhen" ("single weight"). The paperweight formally entered into the study early in the Northern and Southern Dynasties. *Yuan Rongzu* of *History of the Nan Dynasties* records, "Emperor Xiao Daocheng once put a handle beneath the desk and placed an iron-paperweight on top of the desk. Both were large in size and weapon-like, in case something were to happen." From this, it can be seen that the paperweight has already been around for more than 1,500 years.

There are many references about the paperweight in documents. Du Guangting of the Tang Dynasty in *The Strange Stone of Collection of Foreign Matters* writes, "Jinshi (third degree scholars) Li Tiao, from Kuaiji, coincidentally found a tiny stone which was greenish-black, rectangular and with a smooth surface. He used it as a paper weight." Zhang Zi of the Song Dynasty says in his poem, "San Shan Fang Weng gave me some ink and the paperweight is commonly called a golden rhino." Gu Qing of the Ming Dynasty says in his poem, "The patterned wood is made into a rectangular solid tool served for the collator." Paperweights of the Song (960–1279) and Yuan (1279–1368) Dynasties were very rarely passed down. During the Ming Dynasty, paperweights were shaped more like rulers. The top had a handle resembling a creature, matching records. The paperweight with a copper tiger handle, it has a long rectangular base, with a crouching tiger on top. The tiger head carving is exquisite and realistic. The tiger's tail is relaxed and straightforward. The style of the Qing Dynasty (1644–1911) copper paperweights, following the Ming Dynasty (1368–1644), were simultaneously innovative. Following the progress of arts and crafts technology, heavily decorated paperweights began to appear. It could be said that they were a device of both aesthetical and practical value.

This paperweight could be used as a practical device as well as a collectable item. Within the "collectable items circle", red sandalwood and scented rosewood are popular materials used to make paperweights.

This paperweight was originally a piece of aged, ripple-patterned Chinese scented rosewood. The wood grains are unexpectedly clear and the oiliness stands out. To spruce it up somewhat, it was made into a rectangular paperweight. After it was produced, Li himself loved it too much to part with it. The first time I saw it in a brick shop in Tanxin, Beijing, the item's price tag was very high. It was something you could look at, but couldn't have. Afterwards at the Tanxin anniversary auction, I saw it again. The initial price wasn't high. I was really happy to collect the item.

薄壁山水纹花筒

筒体高：23.5 厘米　筒口径：8 厘米　内径：6.5 厘米　肚径：7.8 厘米
筒内深：13.5 厘米　底面直径：8.8 厘米　重：425 克

相思

• 唐 • 王维

红豆生南国，春来发几枝。
愿君多采撷，此物最相思。

此物件是由海南黄花梨民俗老物件打磨翻新而成的花筒，做插花而用。之前已经聊过海南黄花梨老工艺品的来龙去脉，此物件也是其中一个代表。

这只花筒最大特点是薄壁，壁厚仅为一厘米左右。可以想见，当初的整料要挖掉多少心材才得出此物。同时，这只花筒材质细腻，纹理是典型的蟹爪纹走向。环视筒身有如置身于中国水墨写意中的山水画卷，虚幻缥缈，若隐若现，宛若"舟行碧波上，人在画中游"的桂林山水，又如"人游山峡里，宛在画图中"的天门山景。筒身带有大小鬼眼八处，处处惊艳。

花筒置于案几，放入一枝"红豆"，场景引人神往，如若穿行于王维的《相思》之境。

Thin Mountain-Patterned Vase

Vase Height: 23.5 cm　Vase Mouth Diameter: 8 cm　Internal Diameter: 6.5 cm　Body Diameter: 7.8 cm
Vase Interior Depth: 13.5 cm　Base Diameter: 8.8 cm　Weight: 425 g

Yearning

By Wang Wei of the Tang Dynasty

Red beans grew in the South, coming spring, sprouted branches.
Wishing you to pick many, of which I yearned for most.

This vase was polished and refurbished from an old folk southern Chinese scented rosewood object. It is used for arranging flowers. The source of old handicrafts made from southern Chinese scented rosewood has already been discussed in the previous chapters. This object is one of the representatives.

The vase's biggest characteristic is its thin wall. The wall is only about one centimeter thick. You can imagine how much core material was needed to produce it. At the same time, this vase's

material is delicate. The veins incline towards a typical crab-claw-like pattern. Stroking the surface feels as soft and smooth as silk. Viewing the vase's body is like placing oneself inside a Chinese freehand landscape ink painting that is illusory and faintly discernable. It's like the Guilin Mountains—"A boat rowing on blue waves, people swimming in the midst". Or perhaps like the Tianmen Mountain scene—"People roaming mountain valleys winding through the painting". The vase's body has flecks of varying sizes in eight locations, breathtaking in all respects.

If you were to place the vase on a table with "red beans" in it, the scene would be fascinating, as if you were pulled into Wang Wei's poem, *Yearning*.

茶 台

长：30厘米　宽：17厘米　高：6厘米　重：855克

山泉煎茶有怀
唐·白居易

坐酌泠泠水，看煎瑟瑟尘。
无由持一碗，寄与爱茶人。

"茶"字如此组合而成："草"在上头，代表茶，是指东方神草本身；"人"在中间，代表人物，是茶道中心；"木"在底下，代表茶台，是茶道活动承载。寥寥三字的组合，就将茶道的独特意境表现得淋漓尽致。茶台作为茶文化的载体，将品茶人与茶具联系在了一起，创造了茶文化的一种独特意境。

茶台为放置各类茶具的桌台。它可圆可方，可大可小，可精雕可随形，极富自在的美感。当下流行用大的树根料随形而作，这件海黄随形茶台，就是利用一块海黄老油梨根料制作而成。

此件茶台料质温润如玉，表面细腻不见棕眼，且有大片荧光闪闪的水波纹，煞是迷人。茶道高深，各人有各人的体会。约上三五友人，泡上一壶茗茶，以茶会友，岂不美哉？

Tea Table

Length: 30 cm　Width: 17 cm　Height: 6 cm　Weight: 855 g

Reminiscing over Mountain Spring Boiled Tea
By Bai Juyi of the Tang Dynasty

Sitting and pouring cool water,
In the boiling jade water, tea dregs.
Holding a cup without reason,
this feeling is for people who love tea.

The Chinese character for tea, "茶"("cha"), is composed in this way: "草"("cao", meaning "grass"; represented by " ⺾ "in" 茶 ") is written on top. It represents tea. It refers to the magical herb. " 人 "("ren", meaning "person") is in the middle, representing people, the center of tea ceremony; "木"("mu", meaning "tree" or "wood") is at the bottom, representing the tea table, bearing the weight of tea ceremony activities. These three short characters combined display the unique artistic concept of tea ceremony vividly and thoroughly. The tea table is viewed as the vehicle of tea culture, connecting the person tasting the tea with the tea utensils, creating the unique artistic concept of tea culture.

The tea table is where all kinds of tea utensils are placed. It can be round or square, big or small, finely carved or natural—its sense of beauty is in its utmost unrestrained nature. The trend at the moment is to use a big tree root and make the product according to its natural form. A piece of Chinese scented rosewood tree root was precisely what was used to craft this naturally-formed Chinese scented rosewood tea table.

This tea table's quality is gentle like jade. The surface is exquisite, without any flecks. The vast glistening fluorescent ripple-patterned grain is remarkably enchanting. Tea ceremony is profound. Each individual has their own experience. Wouldn't it be beautiful to invite several friends, making a pot of tea, and using tea to make friends?

山水纹盘

直径：18 厘米　重：180.6 克

云际院小池荷花才落，一叶急承之

宋·杨万里

欲落荷花先自愁，如何落后免沉浮。
谁将碧玉圆盘子，和蕊和花一一收。

古代人制作餐具，用料就已经甚为讲究。早在上古，食器就有骨制品、木制品、竹制品、陶制品和青铜制品之分。就盘而言，有陶盘、铜盘和木盘，其中木制餐具极为流行。

盘的尺寸大小不一，形式多样，有敞口、撇口、敛口、洗口、卷沿、板沿、折腰式、葵瓣式、荷叶式、方形转角式和花形攒盘等。在盘子身上，体现了"天圆地方"的美学。

黄花梨制盘，近观山水纹理，清新流畅，线条分明，过渡自然，表面纹理如同一幅优美的水墨画；远观如梦如幻，变化多端，入木三分。

Landscape-Patterned Dish

Diameter: 18 cm　Weight: 180.6 g

Clouds High Over the Pond-side Courtyard, a Lotus Leaf Falls

By Yang Wanli of the Song Dynasty

A lotus flower, longing to fall, worries about herself. How can she fall to avoid bobbing up and down. Who will take a jasper dish, and receive the stamen and the flower one by one.

When people in ancient times produced tableware, the materials used were already extremely delicate. As early as ancient times, the materials used to create eating utensils consisted of bone, wood, bamboo, clay, and bronze. Dishes were produced from clay, bronze, and wood. Tableware made of wood was exceptionally popular.

The diameter of the dish differs depending on a variety of shapes: open-mouthed, flare-mouthed, incurve-mouthed, upturn-mouthed, curl-lipped, flat-lipped, bowed-shaped, sunflower-petal-shaped, lotus-leaf-shaped, square-shaped, flower-shaped bowl set, etc. The body of the dish reflects the aesthetics of "round heaven and square earth".

Upon close inspection of the mountain-patterned veins in the dish made from scented rosewood, one would notice how fresh they are, how they flow smoothly with distinct lines transitioning naturally like a graceful ink and wash painting. From a distance, it appears as a dream, a fantasy, profound and ever changing.

蒜头瓶

瓶径：7厘米　高：23厘米　重：391克

答王司空饷酒诗
南北朝·庾信

今日小园中，桃花数树红。
开君一壶酒，细酌对春风。
未能扶毕卓，犹足舞王戎。
仙人一捧露，判不及杯中。

蒜头瓶是起源于商周时期的一种瓶式样。最早为青铜制，宋朝开始烧制瓷质蒜头瓶，明清时期达到鼎盛。因顶部的形状好似一头大蒜，因此称为"蒜头瓶"，极为贴切。

此种瓶样式，瓶颈细长便于握持，瓶腹圆鼓可以盛装，故也可用作酒器，称之为"温壶"。因为古代酿酒技术还不够发达，酒精度数不够，因此一定要喝很多才会有醉意，故需要酒器容量巨大且需要不断地加温。酒后微醉，拿着酒器来回走动，更需酒器的把握感好，因此蒜头瓶作为酒器就自然讨人喜欢了。

元代后蒜头瓶渐渐由酒器变成陈设器，其饰纹也逐渐丰富多样。由于它的造型独特而又极具观赏性，成为历代皇室必用之物。据说清乾隆帝对此瓶情有独钟，曾多次谕旨烧制。

这件海南黄花梨细口净瓶是由一副插屏座框双拼而成，猜想原先一定是达官贵人家的桌上重器，中间插屏可能是一块纹理绚烂的海黄独板，也可能是一块山水纹理的大理石板，反正能用黄花梨做座框的插屏，作为赏玩主体的插屏一定是惊艳之物。可惜或是年代久远，插屏损毁，或是新主人急功近利，便把黄花梨的座框拆下，拼合做成了现在这个蒜头瓶。

Garlic-Head-Shaped Bottle

Bottle Diameter: 7 cm   Height: 23 cm   Weight: 391 g

Wine for Sikong Wong
By Yu Xin of the Northern and Southern Dynasties

In the small garden, there are many peach trees blooming.
Surrounded by the spring breeze, we enjoy the scenery and ponder the wine.
I can't help drunk Bi Zhuo, but I can dance with drunk Wang Rong.
Even the nectar of the Morning Dew Fairy is probably not as good as the fine wine in my glass.

The garlic-head-shaped bottle was a style originating from the Shang (1600 B.C.–1046 B.C.) and Zhou (1046 B.C.–256 B.C.) Dynasties. The bottle was made of bronze at the earliest, but people began to fire porcelain bottles in the Song Dynasty (960–1279) and it reached its peak in the Ming (1368–1644) and Qing (1644–1911) Dynasties. The shape of the top resembles a garlic. As such, it is called a garlic-head-shaped bottle, which is very vivid. With this style, the bottle neck is slender and easy to hold, and the bottle has a large capacity. Hence, it can also be used as a drinking vessel called a "warm pot". Because the ancient liquor-making technology was not developed enough and the alcohol level was low, people had to drink a lot to get drunk. Therefore, people needed a huge drinking vessel and to constantly heat the alcohol. People walked back and forth with the drinking vessel after getting drunk, so a drinking vessel that could be easily grasped was greatly needed. As such, the garlic-head-shaped bottle was naturally delightful as a drinking vessel.

After the Yuan Dynasty (1279–1368), the garlic-head-shaped bottle gradually changed from a drinking vessel to furnishing, and its decorative patterns became richer and more diverse. Because of its unique and highly ornamental shape, it has become a must-have for all royal families. It is said that Emperor Qianlong of the Qing Dynasty had showed special preference to this kind of bottle and had ordered to make them on many occasions.

This Chinese scented rosewood small-mouthed bottle is made from a pair of screen-seated frames. I suppose it must have been the tabletop appliance of a noble official. The screen insert in the middle may be a gorgeous textured Chinese scented rosewood veneer or a landscape-textured marble slab. The screen of the masterpiece would certainly have been amazing, using the scented rosewood as the frame seat. Unfortunately, the old screen must have been damaged or the new owner was eager for instant benefits, as he removed the frame seat of the scented rosewood and turned it into the garlic-head-shaped bottle.

参考文献

[1] 周默．木鉴：中国古典家具用材鉴赏[M]．太原：山西古籍出版社，2010．

[2] 杨波．黄花梨收藏入门百科[M]．北京：化学工业出版社，2012．

[3] 伍嘉恩．明式家具二十年经眼录[M]．北京：故宫出版社，2010．

[4] 王世襄．明式家具研究[M]．北京：三联书店，2008．

[5] 孙欣，童芸．中国雕刻[M]．合肥：黄山书社，2012．

[6] 白羽．海南黄花梨收藏与鉴赏[M]，北京：新世界出版社，2014．

[7] 徐中玉．古文鉴赏大辞典[M]．杭州：浙江教育出版社，1989．

[8] 钱钟书．宋诗选注[M]．北京：三联书店，2001．

[9] 程千帆．唐诗鉴赏辞典[M]．上海：上海辞书出版社，1986．

[10] 金性尧．唐诗三百首新注[M]．上海：上海古籍出版社，1998．

[11] 把玩艺术工作室．紫砂壶把玩艺术[M]．北京：现代出版社，2015．

[12] 康小兵．文房雅器[M]．石家庄：河北科学技术出版社，2017．

[13] 马未都．马未都说收藏[M]．北京：中华书局，2009．

后记

多年前，由于一次偶然的接触，我喜欢上了木头。此后，黄花梨文玩收藏成为了我最大的心头好。遥想中学时代，我还曾迷恋过集邮，成年后对邮票便意兴阑珊了。倒也并非邮票的世界不够广阔，只是在中年之后，深感对爱好更需谨慎抉择，因为这一爱，基本就是深入而绵长的一辈子。

一花一世界，一木一浮生，无限掌中置，刹那成永恒。这是佛语箴言。如果要在现实世界找到一种到此境地的植物，我便觉得应是黄花梨。它的纹理行云流水，空灵飘逸；质地温润如玉，古韵凝香；气象不温不燥，不亢不卑。加之琥珀色泽，其美典雅而宁静，也符合儒家的中庸之道，像天人合一的思想境界中最形神兼备的形式。因此，黄花梨在很早之前就被古人称为"文木"。

世界上没有两块一模一样的木头，更何况以纹理取胜的黄花梨。将黄花梨雕刻成品后，便将其"文木"的特质升华，成为文化的载体，而文化便是根植在血液里的一种习惯。

现在黄花梨文玩圈内人们大多盯着黄花梨的物理属性，话题脱不开鬼眼、沉水、紫油、降香。但每一个黄花梨文玩把件其实都承载着一种文化寓意。时至今日，黄花梨的内涵从一个树种、一种家具用材，成为在更宽泛的时代背景下，能够寄寓社会文明历史的载体，早已超脱林木科学、商品经济，更不再局限于当代一时的市场发展。因此，本次将物件拍照整理成册，并不在于彰显其市场价值，而是希望从文化的角度给每一个初入此行的朋友做个指引。清中晚期，乱砍滥伐曾经导致黄花梨原料枯竭，致使以黄花梨为主要原料的明清古典家具断层，这已经是一场浩劫。而如果以黄花梨为载体的文玩把件，不再作为特殊的历史属性的凝结，那岂不又是一次灾难。

感谢我的家人，给予我足够的支持和自由的空间，因为这毕竟是一个颇为花钱花时间的爱好；感谢带我入门的陈锐锋先生和万利先生；感谢复旦 MBA 校友梁杰文先生，他杰出的摄影才华是此次藏品集能够面世的重要支持因素。还要感谢复旦大学管理学院孟秋晶老师。同济出版社的编辑老师，她们都给予了我很大的帮助。最后，还要感谢上海交通大学的 Mr. Butt Aaron，为所有的中文资料做了英语翻译，能让更多海外读者了解中国的黄花梨文化，为传播博大精深的中国传统文化添砖加瓦。

最后，希望有更多人能够爱上黄花梨，爱上黄花梨文玩所蕴含的中国传统文化，我也希望能够结交更多有相同志趣的朋友。欢迎添加我的微信号（1904343），一起交流，共同学习。

黄继荣
己亥年冬

黄继荣

图书在版编目（CIP）数据

黄花梨文玩收藏集 / 黄继荣编著 . -- 上海：同济大学出版社，2023.3

ISBN 978-7-5765-0389-0

Ⅰ . ①黄… Ⅱ . ①黄… Ⅲ . ①降香黄檀—收藏②降香黄檀—收藏 Ⅳ . ① G262.5 ② S792.28

中国版本图书馆 CIP 数据核字（2022）第 179931 号

黄花梨文玩收藏集

黄继荣　编著

责任编辑：杨　艳
装帧设计：潘向蓁
责任校对：徐逢乔

出版发行：同济大学出版社
地　　址：上海市杨浦区四平路 1239 号
电　　话：021-65985622
邮政编码：200092
网　　址：www.tongjipress.com.cn
经　　销：全国各地新华书店
印　　刷：上海安枫印务有限公司
开　　本：787mm × 1092mm　1/16
字　　数：349 000
印　　张：14
版　　次：2023 年 3 月第 1 版
印　　次：2023 年 3 月第 1 次印刷
书　　号：ISBN 978-7-5765-0389-0
定　　价：108.00 元